Life In Florida
SINCE 1886

Thonotasassa Rollins College Tampa

EMMA N. GAYLORD

Library of Congress Card Catalog No. 76-100983

Published by

HURRICANE HOUSE PUBLISHERS
14301 S.W. 87th Avenue
Miami, Florida 33158

DEDICATED

TO

PORTIA KEELER GAYLORD

WHO WAS MY CONSTANT PROD AND PROP

TABLE of CONTENTS

Chapter	Page
I.—Thonatasassa.	1
II.—Tampa and School.	7
III.—What We Used.	12
IV.—Water and Fire	18
V.—What We Ate.	24
VI.—What We Lived By.	31
VII.—Sickness and Health.	37
VIII.—Progress and Freezes.	42
IX.—Rollins College, 1897.	47
X.—Faculty and Students.	54
XI.—War, Teaching and Life.	59

INTRODUCTION

For many years I have been urged to write of my early experiences in Florida. I did not respond, for I thought no one would be interested in the life of an average child in a typical American home. But the more I have thought about it the more I have been impressed by the changes that have come about during my lifetime in the way the majority of people lived, and the probability that to many outside my own family the everyday life of that time would be astonishing. But the thing that finally decided me was a sentence by Dr. J. O. Kinnaman in the introduction to his book, DIGGERS FOR FACTS. "Again and again my friends have begged me not to do as my comrade of many years, Dr. Frederick Starr, did—to pass over the great divide without leaving some written record of my investigation."

My memory spans more than three-quarters of the century that has seen the rise of the greatest Empire, the British, and the greatest single nation, the United States, to their zenith, and the beginning of their decline, and the greatest changes in man's environment, science, and mode of living, the astounding present-day running to and fro, and the immeasurable increase of knowledge, not only in the variety and extent of things to be known but also in the numbers of people with sufficient education to know about them. So I have written things down, not necessarily chronologically or in the order of their importance, but as they came to my mind, in the hope they will be interesting.

There has been no researching on my part. If anyone is interested, there are plenty of source books, both fiction and non-fiction. I have mentioned but few names. Biographies are numerous. But I do want to express my thanks to those who have encouraged me, and dedicate this book to them in deep affection.

E. N. G.

CHAPTER I

THONOTOSASSA

Like many other families, we came to Florida for the sake of my father's health which was undermined in the diphtheria epidemic that swept the entire North about 1878, in many cases wiping out whole families. He was one of the group that on October 16, 1885, started to Florida in a little schooner, across Lake Michigan, through the Chicago Canal and Illinois River to the Mississippi River, down it to New Orleans, then across Lake Ponchartrain and the Gulf of Mexico. They reached Tampa three months later, on the 17th of January, 1886, in the middle of a freeze. Bonfires kept people warm along Washington street.

My father was a cabinetmaker. The day after his arrival he started on the interior finish of the First National Bank. He went to work for William Hazen developing a colony at Lake Thonotosassa, fourteen miles northeast of Tampa. The climate agreed with him so well that in the summer of 1886 my parents sold everything they had accumulated in twenty-five years of married life, and started over in Florida. Ma, Rose, aged twelve-and-a-half, Mary, aged ten-and-a-half, and I reached Thonotosassa on October 16, 1886, one year after Pa left Michigan, twelve days before my sixth birthday. My home has been within fifteen miles of there ever since.

We arrived hot and tired from a six days trip by train from our home at Eastport, Michigan, where we left snow on the ground. My sister Rose died at eighty-nine without ever again seeing snow. After many exhausting delays on local trains we arrived in Seffner, Florida, about ten miles east of Tampa, then went in a buckboard the six miles to Thonotosassa. The road followed the route of the present paved highway. But then the road was a bed of sand, "of the firmness and consistency of a featherbed." At Lake Thonotosassa, an Indian name meaning, "lake of flints" Ma picked up a quart jarful of arrowheads in one afternoon. The beach was broad and clean and snow white. It made me heartsick to see it sixty years later, overgrown with water grass and weeds, and a foul dirty gray from defilement by swimmers. When the drainage district was organized, the water from a large area was drained into the outflow and its direction reversed, to the ruin of the lake.

Indians had long since disappeared, also panther and wildcats, except in remote places. Coons and possums were plentiful and bold in raiding chicken coops. Deer kept to the swamps. I still have the horns of a ten-point buck that was killed the last day of the open season, February 28, 1902, so close to the schoolhouse where I was teaching that the children heard the shots and the shouts.

Game of other kinds was plentiful. Uncle Trapnell, my sister Rose's husband, often shot a rabbit for breakfast. I gave Arthur, my oldest grandson, my baby pillow made of quail feathers.

Wild turkey was abundant. For Christmas dinner 1890, Mrs. Ayers bought two for one dollar each. Ma cooked for her boarding house. At a time when good room and board could be had for two dollors and a half a week, she charged seven.

She bought oysters for ten cents a quart. They were smaller than the first ones I saw, while we were living on our farm near Thonotosassa. They were so big two of them filled a cup.

Mullet was the favorite fish. It was about the first thing to come under the protection of the fish and game laws. Farmers went for miles and camped on the shores of the bay, catching them and salting them down by the washtub and barrelful.

It was on such trips that people did most of their salt water swimming and bathing. There were no bathhouses. There were plenty of bushes to provide privacy. Not many women and girls were bold and immodest enough to go in the water with men other than their own family. Old clothes were used for bathing suits. In Tampa the bathing beach was east of the river, between Franklin and Pierce Streets, with clean white sand and unpolluted water.

Gophers and salamanders dug their holes and threw the dirt out in mounds in woods and fields. Riders had to avoid them, for if a horse stepped on one the rider was apt to be thrown and the horse's leg broken. The salamander was the pocket gopher of the dictionary. Our gopher is described as a burrowing land tortoise. Its flesh makes a delicious stew. We children used to stand on their backs, in the hope they would crawl, but they drew tighter into their shells, and remained motionless.

By the time our family settled here a transformation had already begun. Up to the time the first railroad, the South Florida, then the Plant System, and now the Atlantic Coast Line part of the Seaboard Coast Line, reached Tampa in 1884, all commerce was carried by boat or wagon. Key West was the biggest city, population ten thousand, a port of call for vessels from Europe and North, South and Central America. Pensacola was the next largest, Jacksonville the third. The earliest settlers brought household goods and implements with them. To buy anything, they had to go for it by horse or ox drawn wagon, Flour was $20 a barrel, gold. Cornbread took the place of wheat and was their main kind of bread.

Our first home in Florida was an upstairs apartment in a big store building. The older girls slept in a little alcove off the combination living room and kitchen where we ate, and I slept on a little bed Pa made for me in their bedroom. A Mr. Highton had a bedroom opening off our kitchen. Ma bought some flatirons from him. One was a six-pounder, extra good. After I had an electric iron I occasionally used it till the wartime scrap iron drive in 1942.

Our next house was just as unimaginative as most of the houses of that day. There were two rooms under the roof. Ma kept her flour barrel in the space under the stairwell. On the north side, the east end was enclosed for a dining room, and the west end left an open porch. Across the east end of the house a narrow porch had been started. Pa worked at finishing it only in his spare time. When he was working at Thonotosassa he walked the two-and-a-half miles each way, and worked ten hours a day six days a week. Sunday he always respected as the Lord's Day. When he worked in Tampa, he was gone the whole week.

In Michigan, Pa had made all the furniture of maple and cherry grown on the farm. When we came South, Ma sold it all. I remember his telling her, "Never mind, Nancy, I'll nail you a little table together to do you until I can make you a good one." Viva, Rose's older daughter, has the little table he nailed together, while I have the good one, which I watched him make on the back porch in the summer of 1887.

In true Florida fashion, the weather changed overnight, and Sunday morning, October 17, 1886, was clear and nippy. After breakfast Pa peeled a grapefruit with his jackknife and gave each of us a section. The Florida citrus industry was then in its very early infancy. Oranges had been introduced from Spain elsewhere in the state, but, a Spanish sloop had unloaded oranges at Tampa the day before Dade's men started on their fateful march that ended in Dade's Massacre. They camped that night, December 24, 1835, at a spring near Harney called because of the yellow jackets, "The Devil's Punch Bowl." A few years later Lottie Maley's grandfather settled at the southwest corner of Lake Thonotosassa. A "b'ar" killed his favorite hound. With the rest of his hounds he went after the "b'ar", and found orange trees at the Devil's Punch Bowl that had grown from seeds dropped by Dade's men. He blazed the trail back home, then took his mules and dragged out two of the choicest trees. My first orange was from the tree called the "alligator tree" because an alligator had been buried under it. One tree was still bearing at age one hundred four years. It was among the fourteen million trees in this county killed by the freeze of December 12-13, 1962. I understand the first grapefruit was found near Clearwater.

Mr. Hazen was called General, after his cousin, Union General William Hazen, although he disclaimed the title. He induced a good many families to settle in and near Thonotosassa. He sold uncleared land for ten dollars an acre, and was roundly condemned for the exorbitant price. Pa bought ten acres on the installment plan, on which he built a five room story-and-a-half house, board and batten. His partner in the contracting business, James Harris, built the same sized house, clapboards, across the road. Both cleared land and planted orange trees. The place was called Harrisburg. The Harris family consisted of James Harris and his wife Annie, a son about twelve named Pearl (actually his name) and a daughter Rosie, aged five; our family, Henry Dreyer, wife Nancy, daughters Rose and Mary, by then aged thirteen and eleven, and me, aged six-and-a-half—total population nine.

Coming from about as far north as we could on the southern peninsula of Michigan, everything here was different and strange to us: the people, the language, the climate, the trees and flowers, customs of many sorts, and the way of living in general. The difference involved a difficult adjustment or acclimation for both man and beast, for the heat and humidity were almost unbearable. I had no trouble, Rose and Mary very little, but Ma, a strong, vigorous and healthy woman, lay on the sofa most of the time the first year, especially in the summer. Many fine animals, horses, cows and chickens, died in the process.

Many of our neighbors were Confederate veterans. I never heard the Civil War mentioned, though we studied about it in our history classes. The only person who ever showed any animosity was a pretty little girl about my own age, with black curls and snapping black eyes. She would yell at me, "You old Yank, you," and I would yell back, "I'd rather be a Yank than a Cracker like you," without either of us knowing what we were saying. We became fast friends.

As I grew older, more of the older Southerners were willing to talk more freely, and I learned much that made me understand them better and admire them more. Of the first generation that grew up in the South after the war, very few had any schooling.

Negroes owned their farms, and lived with their white neighbors in peace and amity.

Long before I knew anything about the history of Florida, I recognized that there were two distinct racial strains of native Floridians. One had black or dark brown hair and eyes and swarthy skin, with high aquiline nose. The other was blue eyed, with fair hair and skin, and nose more on the order of Grecian. The first were descendants of the conquistadors and the Spanish settlers who followed in their wake. They had come from the original settlements in the upper central and coastal areas. The fair ones had come mostly from Georgia and the Carolinas, principally after the Civil War, and brought with them the language their ancestors had brought from Britain. The words and phrases newcomers found amusing or ridiculous were the purest uncorrupted Elizabethan English.

Their speech was full of proverbs, vivid and pithy. If one was in a hurry and did not want to stop to talk, he was after coals for breakfast, live coals. If a woman rushed to get a garment made, without too much care. "She sewed with a hot needle and a scorched thread." A brief period of extra-strenous activity was a snake killing time. Of the influence of heredity it was said, "If the daddy racks and the mammy racks, you can't expect the colt to trot." One who liked to travel had a loose ankle and an itching foot. I think the best advice Professor Graham ever gave me was. "You can catch more flies with honey than you can with vinegar."

People coming here from the North tried to build cellars, but instead of cool, refrigerator-like places they were hotter than any surface room. Attics were too hot for use except for storage of things heat did not affect. Early settlers, usually young folks, built their houses of readily available material, in this case pine logs. Called a "double-pen house," they had two good sized rooms, fifteen to twenty feet square, with a covered open passageway between, a cool place even in hot weather. In Florida there is always a breeze in the shade. The roof was made of hand riven shingles, and the spaces between the logs covered by hand riven battens, both usually of cypress, a softer wood and easier to split smoothly than pine. Back of this, separate, or connected by a passageway that was often covered, was a smaller structure for cooking and eating. As the family grew shed rooms were added. An old house made one think of a mother hen with her wings spread out to shelter her brood.

These houses were spacious and comfortable. The thick walls kept out the heat in summer. The stick and clay chimney, with clay apron, kept the room warm in winter. Windows were wood shutters, with leather straps in lieu of hinges at the top, held open by a stick. The first glass windows were held up by a stick. The next fastener I recall was a little knob with a spring through the sash into the casing. Doors too were made of boards nailed together, with leather hinges. They were fastened by a piece of board lifted by a rawhide string run often outside a little hole. Hence the expression of hospitality, "The latchstring is out."

Fences were of split rails, or for around yards, of split pickets. By law they had to be "hog tight and bull high," because cattle and roamed at will. It was not until after fighting for years that Florida got the "no fence" law ordering owners to keep livestock fenced in.

Later a cousin of Mr. Harris and a cousin of Mrs. Harris came with their families. There was also a brother of the second Mrs. Harris. Mr. Hazen built a fine three story hotel with a wonderful view of the lake called "The Lakeview." My father built the stairs. One guest commented, "It must have cost Hazen a pretty penny to get that newel post made in New York." The reply was, "No, Mr. Dreyer made it right there in the dining room."

Gradually the boom died. Pa could get work in Tampa, but it meant walking the entire twelve miles to Tampa, or walking six miles to Seffner and taking the train from there, and being home only after dark Saturday night to before daylight Monday morning. Carpenters worked ten hours a day six days a week, so Pa traded our ten acre farm for a $3\frac{1}{8}$ acre tract, which is now the site of the B. C. Graham Elementary School. Shortly after we moved a spur railroad was built, people began commuting, then moved to Tampa, and Thonotosassa stagnated for many years.

CHAPTER II

TAMPA AND SCHOOL

We moved to Tampa November 1, 1889. We started soon after sunrise, our belongings in a rented wagon drawn by two horses. They got us to Tampa shortly after noon. We had our dinner with the Thompsons, who had come from Michigan on the schooner with Pa. Mrs. Thompson served us gopher stew. My outstanding memory of the trip is fording a little stream, rippling and sparkling in the golden morning sun between the trees that arched over its banks.

Two streams crossed Franklin Street, one a block or two south of Whiting Street, small enough to step across. The other was on Jackson Street, with a wooden bridge for wagons, and a separate one for pedestrians. Magbee Springs was the source of a very short stream, not more than three or four blocks long, narrow enough to jump across, but a foot or more deep. A fourth one had its source in a pond on what is now the northwest corner of Woodlawn Cemetery. It crossed Columbus Drive just west of Massachusetts Avenue, and entered the river between the Garcia Avenue and Columbus Drive bridges.

Washington Street was still the main business street. At its foot were the wharves where pretty good sized vessels could moor, like the Lizzie B. Henderson, a three-masted schooner, to and from Mobile. At the corner of Franklin Street was Fribele's dry goods store, two or three steps up from the wooden sidewalk. Across Washington Street, facing east on Franklin, was the First National Bank of Tampa, the first two-story brick building in Tampa. On the remaining corner, facing Franklin, was a three-story brick, the Almeria Hotel. Facing south on Washington, were two or three one story wooden store buildings, with square false fronts up two or three steps from the street. Knight & Wall moved their hardware store to their new brick building on the corner of LaFayette, now Kennedy Boulevard, and Tampa streets in the summer of 1890. I. S. Giddens & Co. had a wholesale and retail staple and fancy grocery store in the corner store at Florida Avenue. Across Florida Avenue a Mr. Ferris had a grocery store. Both of them handled brooms made by Rex Beach's father, also those made by the Lenfestey Broom Co. Quite a few nice residences were east of there.

Business had already started to expand northward. Tibbetts Bros. had an ice cream parlor on the corner of LaFayette and Franklin. Gus Petty had the first music store in Tampa. When Bush built a one-story brick building, and opened a dry goods store, people predicted he was bound to go broke so far out of town. That was the summer of 1890.

Ybor City, the center of the cigar industry, had been founded. The little two-coach streetcar pulled by a wood-burning steam engine, made hourly trips from about the corner of Seventh Avenue, now East Broadway, and Twenty-second Street, down Sixth Avenue, now Henderson Avenue, to Franklin Street, down Franklin to Washington, down Washington to about Pierce Street. There it turned around on a Y that extend a block or two south. It traversed quite a stretch of virgin forest east of Central Avenue. It carried school children from both directions to the big new school at Henderson Avenue and Jefferson Street. The regular fare was five cents, but school children had a special rate, two tickets for five cents. By 1892 electric trolley cars had superseded the steam one.

We settled down in the three-room shack Pa had traded for, hopefully, no doubt. Mary and I were enrolled in the only school in Tampa east of the Hillsborough River at that time, in the big frame building that was moved across Jefferson Street to make way for the brick W. B. Henderson school. It had been built in 1886, two large classrooms on each floor. The school board was severely criticized for building it so big and so far out of town. Schools were organized wherever as many as ten children could be enrolled. Many of them had at least one family that came by wagon from four miles away.

Prof. L. W. Buchholz was the county superintendent then. He earnestly insisted, "I am not a professor," meaning he did not have the education that would have qualified him for that title in Germany. Others have written of the normal school he conducted each summer at Bloomingdale, holding sessions in the Presbyterian church. There he taught the teen-age boys and girls he had found in the various communities, drilled them in the Three R's, psychology and teaching methods. Then after they had gone out to teach, he drove a horse and buggy and visited every school in the county, which then included Pinellas, at least once each term, examining the children and counselling the teacher. He stopped at whatever farm he happened to be near when night overtook him. He spent one night with us. He and Pa stayed up late, conversing in the High German native to both.

Pa had forgotten a good bit of it, but it was a real treat to the homesick younger man to be able to express himself on subjects dear to his heart in language familiar to his lips.

The first term of school I attended was at Lake Thonotosassa in a neat board and batten building. I can recall the names of only fifteen pupils. We had a lovely woman teacher, Miss Lizzie Easton, from Ohio. School had been going about six weeks, so she assigned Lillie Miley, about six months older than I, to tutor me, who became one of my dearest lifelong friends. She became one of the outstanding teachers in the county.

The next school was called Magnolia. It was a poorly constructed little building, with spaces between the crooked logs wide enough to stick a hand through anywhere, a head in many places. The term began in September and ran four months. When it got too cold, we went to a bonfire outside. The next year four-paned windows about two feet square had been set in the north and east walls, and a heater stove put in. We had little or no equipment beyond a three foot by four painted blackboard, none too smooth. But we had a teacher who had attended Oberlin College and kept us on tiptoe to learn more. Charlie Clendenning was so thorough in his teaching that when I came to Tampa I was the youngest child in the third grade, and remained the youngest in the class until I left Hillsborough High. Each father made a desk for his own children according to his own ideas. Ours seated the three of us, about right for Rose and Mary, big for me. Before school started Pa and Mr. Harris blazed a trail a mile through the woods. We went along according to size, Rose leading, Rosie bringing up the rear, chanting, "Single file, Indian style, way to make a path." Drinking water was brought from a nearby farm well, in a cedar bucket with brass hoops.

By the time we entered the Tampa school the school population had so far outstripped the accommodations that the third grade was moved to the little room at the east end of the upper hall. Professor Graham was its only teacher, besides being the principal of the whole school. There were only two students, Arthur Benjamin and Julia Harrison, in the first class that graduated after going the full four years. For at least ten years boys and girls came from as far away as St. Petersburg, Bradenton and Brooksville to the nearest school of that rank. Summerlin Institute at Bartow drew from an equally large area. Those two, and St. Leo at San Antonio, near Dade City, were the only schools giving high school instruction south of the Rollins Academy at Winter Park.

The Catholic church had a little chapel on the site of the present Sacred Heart. Their music department was noted for the excellence of its instruction.

The First Baptist church was on the southeast corner of Tampa and Madison Streets, where the back end of the First National Bank is now. They moved from there about 1895 to Plant Avenue across from their present site. The old building was used for classrooms for Hillsborough High School the winter of 1896-97. My second-year Latin class, three boys and two girls, met in the belfry.

Our recreation was like that of children everywhere. There were always trees to climb and fences to walk, and trees in which to hang swings and ropes to climb. There were plenty of dead limbs to make walls and partitions for playhouses in the clean sand under the trees, and pine cones, acorns and broken pieces of dishes to furnish them with. Dolls made of corncobs and shucks answered every purpose. Rag dolls were apt to be favorites. Really nice "store bought" ones were of wax, bisque, and china (heads, hands and arms, feet and legs), with bodies stuffed with cotton or sawdust. Wax melted in hot weather, and once their features ran there was no more beauty in them. My favorite toy was a little tin horse and wagon. Tin dishpans made resounding drums. Pine cones could be knocked around with a stick. Smilax vines made good jump ropes. I often skipped the mile home from school not much faster than I would have walked. Periwinkle blossoms were better than any pipe for blowing bubbles.

At school, where there were enough children together, we played what we called baseball. The size and shape of the field were determined by the location of the pine trees we used for bases. Balls were of patiently saved grocery twine, with a cover of old sock sewed around it. If we could get a rubber core of old overshoe or fruit jar ring, so much the better. The ball traveled farther through the air and bounced higher and more times. If caught on or before the third bound, it was an out. The runner had to be hit with a thrown ball. A wild throw could insure a home run any time. The bats were either straight pieces of tree limbs or of 1″ x 2″ board, whittled round at one end for the hands to grasp, the other shaped more like a paddle than a bat, which the girls preferred. Everybody played, from the first graders to the oldest fifth grade boys. Some of the scores were fantastic, such as 36 to 0. Such a thing as an umpire had never been heard of.

Ma frequently took us to spend the day with the Mileys. Once we left the older girls to amuse themselves with ladylike occupations, while Lottie and I went to the calf pen. I think a moving picture of us two little barefoot eight-year-old girls firmly holding the tails of two eight-months-old calves while they galloped round and round the rail fenced pen until the aforesaid girls turned loose the aforesaid tails from sheer breathless exhaustion would be as entertaining to spectators as it was to us.

One or more circuses came to Tampa every winter, and people brought their children from miles around to see them. A dog and pony show came several years in succession. Many good one-night shows came. Many musicians and lecturers of high caliber came here because of our warm climate.

We had sewing circles, literary clubs, debating societies, family and neighborhood parties, and just spontaneous getting together for a pleasant time. Many evenings were spent at home, with someone reading aloud books by the great authors of English literature.

From birth girls were taught to make themselves attractive. Babies had gold rings tied on their tiny fingers by a ribbon around the wrist; their tiny ears were pierced for "yur bobs." Even the poorest girl had a box of face powder, chalk white in color. If she applied it too lavishly she was teased about having stuck her head in the flour barrel. But use it she did. No doubt it added to her physical comfort and mental poise. No lipstick or rouge was ever used. No decent, self-respecting woman would have made such a painted Jezebel of herself. She wore a sunbonnet that protected face and neck, and wrist length sleeves, and old stockings over her hands when obliged to work in the sun.

Most older men wore full patriarchial beards. The younger ones were enormously proud of their handlebar moustaches. Even those who were clean shaven thought a once a week shave sufficient. The razors were old-fashioned straight ones, kept sharp on a leather strap. Safety razors were a heartily welcomed invention. A specially designed cup had a lip across one side to keep the moustache from getting into the coffee. All men kept their hair cut reasonably short. One with shoulder length hair was an object of scornful stares. A woman who for any reason, such as severe illness, had had to cut her hair considered herself disgraced.

If a girl was one of the fortunate few who had naturally curly hair she was the admiration and envy of her mates. They tried to make up the deficiency by dampening their hair and rolling it on curlers made of cloth, paper, strips of old glove or even old shoetop. Later there was a curler that was placed in the top of the lamp chimney and heated enough to impress the curl but not scorch the hair. It worked somewhat on the principle of a pair of scissors, a round steel rod fitting into a hollowed out one, with wooden handles.

Mothers taught their daughters all the homemaking arts and crafts they knew, so that when a girl was married at from sixteen to eighteen years she was prepared to preside over her own home with confidence and dignity.

By modern standards, we would have been considered ill-housed, ill-clothed, underfed, grossly under-privileged. But we didn't know it, and lived about as happily as folks do now and raised fine families. I doubt very much if we suffered any more hardship and privation than pioneers did everywhere; less, probably, because we did not have snow and ice and blistering hot winds to contend with. We were self-supporting, self-respecting, and self-reliant. We provided not only for our daily necessities, but also for our own entertainment. We had our share of joys and sorrows, of achievements and failures. The old timers met the exigencies of life with courage and fortitude equal to the occasion.

Where there was so much ignorance there was bound to be the superstition and vice that always accompany it, but I did not come in contact with it. There was a high moral atmosphere surrounding the young folks like a protecting shield. I am really sorry for the young folks that are growing up now.

CHAPTER III

WHAT WE USED

Native horses were rather small ponies, many showing by their conformation they were descendants of those brought by the Spaniards. Shoes were not needed. The sand kept their hoofs worn down smooth and even. They were poor and unkempt, not much more than walking skeletons. Their usual feed was corn on the cob, which they shelled with their own teeth. Forage was provided by sun dried corn leaves, called fodder. Soil deficiency, mosquitoes, fleas and ticks, contributed to the general lack of well-being. Their manes and tails were matted with cockleburs. Grooming was done by casual rubbing with crocus sacks.

The first wagons I remember were Studebakers. Harness was the bare minimum of bridle (bit, cheek piece, throat latch and crown piece), collar, hames, and saddle and bellyband. Chain was used for traces, rope for reins. Breeching was not needed in our level terrain. I never saw a two-wheeled ox-cart except those drawing logs to the sawmill.

Some few women, especially of the older generation who frequently had to ride for their lives from the Indians, were expert bareback riders. Grandma Miley rode sideways, whether on a sidesaddle or any saddle at all, I do not remember. With her market basket of fresh vegetables for sale on her left arm, she rode up to the fence, and after Ma had made her purchase, went galloping off again. Fires kept the underbrush burned off, so one had a virtually unobstructed view as far as the eye could see.

Cattle were carefully marked and branded, but horses were not. Most farmers had only one, or at most four or five. Whenever and wherever a man saw a horse he wanted or met someone who wanted his, and was willing to trade even or give five or ten dollars boot, the transaction was concluded then and there.

Oxen were not traded so casually. It was genuine hard work, strenuous exercise, to break them in. By the time they were tamed and trained enough to make them tractable and trustworthy, a man thought he had something worth keeping. A good team was of working strength for from fifteen to twenty years.

Cows also were small, descendants of Spanish stock. Their horns were large, running fifteen to eighteen inches, with heavy bases two to three inches in diameter, giving their heads a masculine look for offense and defense. Alligators took a heavy toll of calves. All had marks and brands registered in the county courthouse, and known by heart to settlers. But they roamed the woods and fended for themselves and herded together as they chose. Calves were given the marks and brands of the cow that suckled them, until their horns were so big they kicked them away in self-defense. They usually had a calf every third year. The herd usually doubled in three years. It was a profitable industry, especially after the human population increased. Cuba was a good market from early days, especially immediately after the Spanish-American War.

Big cattlemen gave farmers the privilege of penning all the cattle they wanted to for two or three months in the spring, which served the dual purpose of fertilizing the garden patches and keeping the cattle from being totally wild. During the season the farmers had all the milk they wanted. Cows were turned out from the calves in the pen to graze in the morning. Towards evening they were rounded up and penned. The men carried braided leather whips ten to fifteen feet long, on a wood stock a foot or so long. An expert—and boys were proficient by the time they were fifteen—could swing the whip and snap it with a crack like a rifle shot; hence the nickname, "Florida Cracker." At the first crack the cattle began moving towards the pen.

At night the calves were allowed to suck all the milk, then were turned out to graze. In the morning the calf was allowed to suck on the left side till the milk was "down," then was held off by rope while the milker stood on the right side and milked into a quart cup held in the left hand. It took practice to do either milking or holding. After taking a cupful or so, the milker moved to another cow and another, until there was enough milk in the bucket hung on the fence. The calves finished the stripping. There was no refrigeration. The milk was allowed to stand until it clabbered (one of the words strange to us: we had called it loppered milk), then was churned by shaking in a half-gallon (we called it two-quart) fruit jar. The product was pale cream or white, soft and spongy, not palatable. By early May the cows could get a weed to eat that made the curd tough and leathery, so the cows were turned loose till next penning season. The Crackers did not care for butter, and preferred buttermilk to sweet milk.

When Northerners wanted to have milk all the time, they had to teach a cow to eat by putting cut potato vines in a box with bran. It took patience to teach a cow to allow the milker to sit on a box and use both hands.

Cattlemen complained bitterly that the range was getting poorer all the time, yet every year they set fires to burn off the dead grass. As we sat at dinner one Sunday we looked out the door in time to see a wall of fire coming over the rise (called a hill). We cut young pine saplings, and beat it out just before it reached our fence.

I can never forget the burning of Simmons Hammock, nor the date on which it ended, May 24, 1889. Mrs. Harris had invited several of us neighbor children to spend the day with Rosie in honor of her sixth birthday. For three days the air had been filled with smoke and ashes. The fire started on the east side of Thonotosassa Lake, and swept west and south unhindered. After dinner we children walked the mile or so to a point where we could see the fire. It came as fast as a horse could run, the flames leaping from one treetop to another, while the flames from the underbrush caught on the bark and rushed up with a WHOOSH to the top, from there to leap to the next top. It was an awesome sight. It finally reached the edge of the hammock, where the underbrush had already been burned, so the fire died from lack of fuel. The hammonck has never been restored.

Even after it became unlawful to set fires and let them run, there were those who defended the old practice, on the ground that it destroyed snakes, which it undoubtedly did.

Very few sheep were kept. The climate was not cold enough to make good fleece. The buzzards ate unprotected lambs. But a good word can be said for buzzards. Repulsive looking, ungainly on the ground, majestic in soaring flight, without their efficient scavenger service unsanitary conditions everywhere would have been far worse than they were.

Goats ran wild and were hunted like game.

The razorback hog was as lanky and long-nosed as he has been pictured to be. Their ears were marked with the same marks as cattle, but they were not branded. They ran wild in the woods, eating whatever they could find, acorns, nuts, berries, persimmons, and were not at all averse to breaking a fence and feasting on corn and sweet potatoes. As wanted for food, they were caught with dogs and penned and fattened. In spite of their formidable tusks, which they used to defend their young, alligators and wildcats ate many pigs. Sows were vigilant mothers, with litters of ten or twelve little pigs.

Most families had an axe, a saw, a froe and a maul, for splitting rails, a hatchet that served as a hammer, a screw driver, a file and a grindstone, and that was all. I used to feel sorry for the women who sharpened their knives on the stovepipe, until I learned by experience that a stovepipe is the finest kind of carbon steel sharpener. Hoes were heavy, of the type made by plantation blacksmiths. Tables were made of boards nailed together. Benches, that would seat more than chairs, were frequently made of hewn logs. Chairs were usually of hickory, straight up-and-down backs, two or sometimes three slats across them, seats of cowhide hair side up, about the most uncomfortable things imaginable.

Wire potato mashers had been invented. Most women used the wooden ones they already had. I have often used the one my husband's mother brought from Michigan. It is a pestle about ten inches long, turned from one piece of maple. Ma had one a little larger, that Pa made for her from maple grown on the farm. Southern women used a three-tined steel table fork, slowly and laboriously mashing and whipping till the potatoes were creamy and fluffy.

Rotary eggbeaters with two blades had been invented. Many particular cooks thought egg whites must be beaten with a silver fork. Mrs. Ayers was one of them. Every Saturday she baked an angel's food cake. On a big platter I beat a dozen eggwhites with a silver fork till they were stiff, and my arm too. Mrs. Ayers always saw to it that I had a piece in my school lunch on Monday. Ma used the yolks to bake other kinds of cake. Uncle Trapnell said bakery bread was "wasp's nests." To Northerners, bread meant "east bread" (yeast bread) also called light bread by Southerners, but seldom made. Wild yeasts got into the dough, and results were uncertain. Everyone used cornmeal. Biscuits were made for virtually every meal. Flour was kept in a wooden trough holding a half-peck or more. In a depression in the middle the dough was made, each biscuit pinched off and rolled in the hands until smooth, as evenly sized as if made by machine. The leavening was bicarbonate of soda if sour milk or orange juice was used. Sweet milk or water called for "baking powders," in those days, cream of tartar and soda. After we came to Tampa we bought the first Royal and Rumford baking powder, but most Southern women preferred Clabber Girl.

Knives and forks for table use were of poor quality steel, with wood or horn handles. Butcher knives were of good steel. If a man was handy enough, he could make an excellent knife out of a worn-out file. Very few women had paring knives. They used butcher knives for all purposes. Tin measuring cups were quart, pint, half pint and gill. Their capacity varied with the manufacturer, until the federal government established standards for both weights and measures. Rollingpins were unknown. The hands or a round bottle were used. After the railroads came, stores stocked the pins, but very few were sold. I am still using the one Mrs. Walters bought at Kress' in 1905 for ten cents. Pa made one for Ma of maple grown on our farm. Rose's daughter Viva had it the last I knew of it.

Analine dyes came on the market about the time we came to Florida. Indigo was still used, a very dark blue. Usually the calico was indigo background with white figures or flowers in pretty designs. The white parts dropped out in holes long before the cloth was worn out. Dishrags were really made of rags in those days. There was a common saying that when the dishrag got to be a yard long it was time for the cook to get a new dress. Dishes were rinsed and left to drain.

House brooms were made of saw palmetto leaves, a half dozen or so tied together. Cracks were wide enough for the dirt to fall through. Yards were kept clear of grass, swept clean with brush brooms by the women or girls.

Women did their own sewing. Cotton thread was the same then as now, if anything smoother and evener, and certainly freer of knots. Thread was the familiar J. & P. Coats and Clark's O.N.T. Sizes ran 8, 12, 16, 20, 24, 30, 36, 40, 46, 50, 60, 70, 80, 90 and 100. Forty was the size generally used for garment making, also for quilting, and twenty-four for buttonholes and sewing on buttons. The only time I ever saw 100 used was by Miss Anita Bibbins, head of the music department at Rollins. She made a filmy collar of the sort of lace made by nuns in Belgium. The first lithographed card I remember was one advertising O.N.T. thread, a five- or six-year-old girl sitting on a stool, her needle held out at arm's length on her thread, with the legend, "Get out of the way, Mother, I want to sew."

Black and white were the only colors used very much. Dye seemed to rot the fibers. The colors were dull and unattractive. A two hundred yard spool cost five cents. Silk thread came on fifty yard spools that cost ten cents. Silk could be dyed successfully, and came in colors to match the fabric, as now.

Needles and pins were as good as any obtainable now, safety pins also. About as far back as I can remember, they began putting a safety guard on them, to keep the cloth from getting caught in the coil. Buttons have existed, I suppose, from the dawn of history. Iridescent mother-of-pearl ones cost about twice as much as the commonly used ones of porcelain and mollusk shell. Brass was used for those on military uniforms. Snap fasteners that could be sewed on, and the DeLong hook and eye with its "See that Hump?" came about 1895. About the same time seam binding and bias tape with folded edges were introduced, along with inexpensive machine-made lace edging.

The wonderful process of mercerizing cotton, that made it look like silk, came about the time I went to Rollins in 1897. I saw my first blouse made of it while I was there. It was delicate blue in color, a very pretty garment indeed.

Patterns for embroidery were perforated paper and stamped with powder, easily blurred and rubbed off the cloth in working. One popular design for pillow shams, done in outline stitch in Turkey red cotton thread (about the only color that would not run or fade), was the picture of a woman sleeping, with the legend, "I slept and dreamed that life was beauty," and for the companion sham a woman sweeping, with the legend, "I woke, and found that life was duty." They were made of bleaching (bleached muslin), starched and ironed, and spread over the pillows placed on their edges at the head of the bed during the day, carefully removed and folded at night. When we were married, my husband still had the pair his mother had made.

Silk embroidery thread in all colors that came on tiny spools an inch in diameter and half an inch high containing ten feet could be bought for one cent a spool.

Ma had a piece of quarter-inch thick wood, the edges cut with different curves, with which she could cut to measurement a pattern for any garment by following the printed instructions that came with it. I remember her making a black alpaca coat for Pa to wear to a Fourth of July picnic at Lake Thonotosassa.

By the time we came to Tampa we could get tissue paper patterns; but the instructions were meager, the measurements inaccurate, requiring a good deal of skill to make them fit. Good dressmakers were in demand, and made good incomes. The highest compliment that could be paid was to say a woman looked as if she had been melted and poured into her dress. Ready-to-wear garments were made for men and women of ideal proportions, and seldom fitted.

Sewing machines had already been improved to very much like the non-electric ones are now, except that to wind the bobbin the thread had to be guided by hand. Agents went throughout the countryside, carrying a demonstrator machine in the back of their buggy. They took orders, delivered them, then came back at regular intervals to collect installment payments, make repairs and adjustments, and supply needles, thread and bobbins. The Singer was a favorite.

Shoes were usually either black or white leather, with high tops that came two or three inches above the ankle, and either laced or buttoned with buttons an inch or so apart. By the time a shoe was broken in the leather was usually pliable enough to be buttoned with the fingers and the buttonhook abandoned. Prices ranged from fifty cents a pair for infants' to five dollars for men's dress wear. Most of them were either high topped or ankle height.

The most commonly worn headgear was the sunbonnet. Some were of pretty cloth with a little ruffle around the face. Most of them were of coarse cotton cloth called homespun, although it was made in mills somewhere else and shipped into Florida. They were made of two thicknesses of cloth, so they could be stiffly starched. Sometimes they were stitched and slats of pasteboard slipped into the slots and they were uncomfortable.

For ordinary wear for men and women and children hats were made of bleached cabbage palmetto leaves. They had to be cut at just the right stage of development, fully grown, but before the "pleats" had fully separated. They were hung in the shade to dry and bleach to a rich cream color. They were stripped with a pin into strips about one-fourth inch wide at the butt end, wrapped in a damp towel to keep them pliable, and braided. For hats for everyday use the plait was plain, but for dress wear skilled women could make half a dozen or more variations.

CHAPTER IV

WATER AND FIRE

Some few families got their water from a nearby spring or branch. Most of them had dug wells, walled with pine boards that flavored the water for months. Those that went through clay or rock were walled only till the clay or rock was reached. Good underground streams of palatable water were usually found at a depth of thirty to forty feet. The nearer to the seacoast the greater was the mineral content and worse the taste. Many of the springs were rank with sulphur and other minerals, which made the water highly medicinal. They became health resorts. The ones at Safety Harbor were first named Green Springs for a man of that name who was brought here on a stretcher. He fully recovered and lived many years; a Methodist preacher, I think, who rode the Thonotosassa circuit when we lived there.

Water was drawn from the wells in a bucket on a rope. Sometimes it was simply lowered and pulled up, but usually the rope was passed through a pulley hung to a piece of two-by-four on a frame over the well, two or three feet higher than the top of the curb. Sometimes it was wound up by a windlass, but it was usually pulled up hand over hand. I remember seeing only one sweep in Florida.

Sometimes there was a little roof over the frame of the well, usually not. Inasmuch as ground water in Florida remains an even 72 degrees the year around, it felt cool in summer and warm in winter. If a well got too full after heavy rain, it was emptied, any trash removed, and allowed to refill with fresh clean water from the underground stream that supplied it.

During the rainy season there was plenty of water. In the early years, from the middle of May to the middle of September we could depend on a good rain every day. We always had every year what I called a "six day storm." They are now called hurricanes, and frequently pass us by, depriving us of needed rain by so doing. During the rainy season water was caught in above ground cypress cisterns or rain barrels, to help out during the dry spells. It was easier to draw a bucketful or dip it from under the eaves than to pull it up from the well and carry it to the house. It was not used for cooking or drinking. Wiggletails flourished after the weather turned warm in the spring. Straining through a cloth got them all out. For months at a time water stood all over the flatwoods till it soaked back into the ground. Ponds were plentiful. Springfield lakes and sinkholes abounded.

After railroads made pipe available, open wells were superseded by driven ones with pitcher pumps. They were driven by a block of wood attached to a rope passed through a pulley fastened to a rough tripod made of two-by-fours, pulled up and dropped, pulled up and dropped, hour after hour, day after day, until a sufficient stream of good water was reached. It was wonderfully convenient to have them close to the house; even on the porch, with a wooden sink.

Steam pumps came several years before electric ones. The Tampa Water Works pumped water from a well outside a little red brick building still standing on the northeast corner of Henderson Avenue and Jefferson Street. Its first tank had long icicles hanging from it at the time of the Big Freeze, February 8, 1895. The waterworks plant was moved to Magbee Springs about 1900.

I saw my first faucet at the schoolhouse across the street, where the former W. B. Henderson Elementary school now stands. Water to make lawns brought lawn mowers, like the ones pushed around still by those who can't afford gasoline or electric ones. Gasoline engines were adapted for use on pumps after they had been invented for automobiles.

After there were railroads to bring the heavy machinery, sawmills were set up wherever there was enough demand for lumber to warrant their erection. The same steam boiler also powered a grist mill or even a rice thrasher. The trees were cut down, the tops and limbs left to dry and make a fire hazard. The logs were attached by a chain to an ox cart and dragged to the mill leaving ruts ten or twelve inches deep. The mills used the bark slabs for their own firewood or sold them for home fires. Mr. T. J. Caruthers had a mill for cutting and splitting wood for use in homes. It was first located on the Seaboard Air Line (then the Florida Central & Peninsular) railroad, near the homestead of the Bell family for whom Bell Street is named. Later he moved over on the river near the Fortune Street bridge. Heating was done by open fireplaces for many years after cast and sheet iron heaters were available.

Only one of our neighbors was still cooking on a fireplace when we came here, and the next year she had a good cookstove. Fuel was no problem. Pine cones were ideal kindling, to be picked up anywhere, excellent for a quick brief fire, for frying an egg or boiling a cup of water. For wood, all a man had to do was go out in his field and fell a dead tree and chop and split it into the desired size. When land was cleared the trees were girdled and left to die. When they were cut down, the stumps were left. Plowing was done between and around them. Hence arose the saying that more corn was grown in crooked rows than in straight ones. Plows were small and could cut only a shallow furrow. Deep plowing would have destroyed what fertility there was in the thin top soil. When former Northern farmers began clearing land, they dug a hole at one side of the stump, built a little fire, and left the stump to burn out. It was so full of resin that the fire burned till the last vestige of the stump was consumed. Sawmills left the stumps untouched.

Kerosene cost twenty-five cents a gallon, at that time the going hourly rate for skilled carpenters. There was then no use for gasoline and very little for naptha, so they were left in the kerosene, making it dangerously explosive unless used with great care. Lamps were small glass ones. Chimneys were easily broken and expensive, ten cents apiece, so were seldom used. The flame just flickered and smoked.

In the summer of 1889 Ma had the agency for the Wanzer lamp. It was nickel plated brass, held about a pint of oil, and used a Number 2 wick, about one-and-a-half inches wide. Near the bottom of the hollow upright handle was a spring wound by a key like a clock key, that turned a horizontal fan with little blades like an electric fan, that blew a steady flow of air on the wick. The result was a smokeless flame that gave an unflickering mellow light, excellent for reading. It had a narrow ledge around the biggest part of the bowl, on which could be set an iron ring connected by three upright rods of 3/16 inch wire about six inches long to a similar ring. Over this could be cooked small quantities, water heated, coffee made, eggs fried.

In 1889 I saw my first kerosene stove. It was made of sheet iron, the bowl rectangular, about two inches wide by six inches long by two inches deep, holding about a pint of oil, and using a wick about four inches wide. The chimney was sheet iron with a little mica window in one side, so the flame could be seen. The first kerosene heaters were the round portable ones with round wicks. They heated very well, but if care was not taken to keep them turned down they could in minutes smoke walls and ceilings that took hours to clean up.

The gas plant in Tampa was erected some time around 1890. Its service was extended to the northeast area of Tampa in 1924. My first gas stove was a combination gas and wood range bought from Montgomery Ward of Chicago by catalog. By the time the gas stove needed replacing, electric stoves had been improved.

Cookstoves and ranges were sold by agents, also pots and pans. Most of the ranges were equipped with big copper reservoirs holding fifteen to twenty gallons, which gave an abundance of hot water. Early pots and pans were made of tin or sheet or cast iron. Next came cast iron lined with enamel, then gray enamelware. Aluminum was one of the curiosities of the Chicago World's Fair of 1893.

I have cooked on open fires outdoors, when camping, on charcoal furnaces, on kerosene and gasoline stoves, as well as gas and electric. But my sister Rose was the only woman I ever knew who had ever learned to cook on a wood stove who did not prefer it to any other kind. When the weather is cool enough so I can cook my meals without cooking myself, I still prefer a wood stove, which I have always had in addition to gas and electric through the years. Later, my little cookstove was an object of curiosity. One middle aged woman told me it was the first one she had ever seen. My husband made a six-inch high platform to stand it on, to raise it to comfortable working height for me. I'm not a fire worshiper, but the waste heat for cooking our breakfast is most acceptable to our bodies on cold mornings. Finally the time came when it was advisable to do away with the stove. Our son Stanley wired it so it could be cooked on electrically while it lent "atmosphere."

Arc lights for street lighting had been installed in a very small area along Franklin and LaFayette Streets some two or three years before we came to Tampa. Incandescent lamps for homes came about the same time. Only a handful of people had them. Electric street cars began running in 1891 or 1892, after completion of the powerhouse at the dam. The electric company built the pavilion and pier at Ballast Point, to which they ran a double-decker car four round trips a day. On special occasions such as holidays the service was increased to take care of whatever crowds there might be. It was the elite recreation center for many years, a paradise for picnickers, bathers, fishermen, and those who just wanted a quiet restful hour in a lovely park.

If the Salvation Army rule for judging a family's worthiness for help were applied, that is, their effort to keep clean, most Cracker families would surely have qualified. They could buy lye in cans. They saved their grease and made soap. It removed grime, likewise skin. Men shaved with it. Women washed their hair and the children's with it. Clothes were washed with it. White ones remained white. Colored ones soon were bleached. The first laundry soap that could be bought here was yellow. I have forgotten the brand name. Octagon soon joined it. Ivory came about the same time, Fels-Naptha about 1895. Fine Castile soap, and other good toilet soaps, were always obtainable in Tampa. The first washing powder was a white one called Pearline, just about as caustic as lye. Even for years after Pearline and Gold Dust, a yellow powder, were easily available, soap for boiling clothes was sliced into the boil pot as needed. Soft soap was made by heating the soap with a little water till it made a soft jelly, easily dissolved.

The big turpentine stills let their employees bring their own bottles and get all the fresh turpentine they wanted for household uses. A cake of white scouring soap called Sapolio was soon followed by Bon Ami. Pots and pans were scoured with sand, always available in unlimited quantities.

When it came to floors, clean white sand was brought from the creek bed, spread on the floor, rubbed with the lye soap, then scrubbed with a brush made from a cross section of palmetto log, with the pulp pounded out to leave stiff fibers an inch or so long. Sometimes the brush was made with a heavy block of pine set with corn shucks. Scrubbing was done on hands and knees. The sand and suds were rinsed off and the spotless floor dried by pushing a "croker" sack around with the feet (mops were unknown.)

Washtubs and washboards were unknown until Northerners introduced them. A hollowed-out log, with a hole bored in one end for a drain, was set near the well under a shelter or on the bank of the creek. Water was heated and clothes boiled in a big iron pot. Instead of rubbing on a board, a "battling stick" was used. The wet and soaped article was laid on a wood block, beaten with a two-foot smooth stick, turned from time to time till all the surface dirt was pounded out. I don't remember that the treatment was any harder on the fabric than rubbing on a board, nor any harder on the washwoman. Pa made Ma a washboard of heart pine she used for many years after they could be bought in stores. Later the wood was covered with sheet zinc, still later with brass, then the rubbing surface was made of corrugated glass.

The first washing machines are now museum pieces. Rose got a 1900 Whirlpool washer, a round tub like an ordinary washtub, with a spring underneath attached to the frame. The tub was pulled by an upright handle on one side, and pulled back by the spring underneath. It could wash more clothes at a time, but took a strong arm and stout back to operate it. Pa made us what we called a pounding barrel, a straight sided barrel slightly smaller than a flour barrel. A round board with holes and a handle like a broomstick, could be lifted up and down on the clothes, pulling the clothes up and forcing the water through the holes, the forerunner of suction cup electric machines. It was fun to stand on the rim of the barrel, raising the block and letting it fall, swishing the suds up as the clothes were cleansed. Hand wringers were brought by many from the North, but never had much vogue among the natives.

It was commonly said, "I'd rather wash than starch and iron." When the clothes were washed they were spread on fences or bushes to dry. Clotheslines and pins came later. Those not to be ironed were folded and put away "rough dry." In those days men wanted their shirt fronts and separate collars and cuffs as stiff as boards. By the time we came commercial corn starch was available, in big lumps.

One time Ma made starch out of cassava root. The root had to be peeled and grated, the starch washed out and let settle, and drained and dried. This method of manufacture made a starch that worked all right, but the process was too tiresome and tedious to be worth while. Any of them had to be made with care, just the right proportion of starch and water, boiled to just the right temperature, till it bubbled "fine like spit."

The actual ironing was done with regular flatirons, heated by standing on their heels in front of an open fire, or on a charcoal furnace. This was a bucket made of fire clay, the outside covered with sheet iron. Horizontally across the middle was a partition with a half dozen or so holes through it. Below it was a small opening in the side wall, covered with a sheet iron plate which could be moved up or down to regulate the draft on the charcoal on top of it. If the charcoal smoked it made a gummy streak on the face of the iron difficult to get off. If any rubbed off on the garment being ironed, that had to be washed again.

Just about the time we came here there was introduced an iron I called a steamboat iron. Its face was a trifle larger than an ordinary flatiron. It had a compartment to hold the charcoal, with a tin spout like a stovepipe elbow, but only about an inch in diameter and two inches long, on the top of the front end, pointing away from the user, as a vent. The handle was wood, well insulated from the heat. They were considered very nice. Some beautiful ironing was done with them.

The ironing was done on a folded sheet or quilt laid on a table. Ironing boards were introduced by settlers from the North, but were slow to be adopted. I am still using the one my husband made from the cypress board given us for a wedding present by Uncle Will and Aunt Annie Burgess, the people he had boarded with for five years before we were married.

CHAPTER V

WHAT WE ATE

The variety of food was limited. Most families had a little garden in which they raised vegetables enough for their own use, saving their own seed from year to year. Pa and Mr. Harris got most of their seed from W. Atlee Burpee & Co. of Philadelphia. D. M. Ferry & Co. of Detroit and Hastings of Atlanta also sent out big catalogs, with gorgeous lithographs. Grocery and general stores had a few packets of the most commonly used seeds. Dime stores about the turn of the century sold seeds, bulbs and living plants later. People had to learn that some northern favorites will not grow in Florida.

Collards were the most usual kind of greens, with stalks four or five feet high. One enterprising man always planted two patches, one on high ground, the other on low, so whether the season was wet or dry he had one good garden. Irrigation solved that problem. Artesian wells began to be sunk in the Ruskin region early in this century. Wells and especially constructed pumpers came later. Irish potatoes could be grown here only in the winter. Given sufficient water, cabbage and lettuce made firm heads. String beans then had sure-enough strings. Cowpeas were liked far better. Black-eyed peas came later. They, and beans left whole, cabbage cut in quarters, turnip and mustard greens, usually were overcooked by boiling with a big chunk of white or smoked bacon till the bacon was tender. Cole slaw was chopped in a wooden bowl with a one-or two-bladed chopping knife. Scallions were eaten alone or cut up with tomatoes or cucumbers. Green corn was called "roas'n yurs" (roasting ears) and greatly relished. It was boiled on the cob, and cut off the cob and fried or creamed, but I never did see any roasted. Dry corn was taken to the mill and ground, the miller taking his pay out of the grist. What remained was brought home and shaken in sieves, the fine grains falling through the sieve being used for corn-bread. The coarser grains were cooked as grits or hominy. The sieves were of fine wire mesh across a round wooden box like a cheese box, of varying sizes, and used for flour, too. Rotary flour sifters were invented about the time we came here.

Peanuts were called goobers. Chufas were raised for hog feed. By the time a bunch of hogs had rooted out all the sweet little hard-shelled nutty flavored tubers the ground had been thoroughly plowed, ready for another planting. Sweet potatoes were of the variety known as "Providence." They came up as volunteers and were about the first vegetables Georgians had after the devastation of war, and were named Providence because it was felt God had provided them. In the fall they were dug and stored in a "bank," a shallow hole in the ground varying in size according to need, lined with pine straw, covered with boards making an inverted V over them, then the boards thatched with pine straw to shed rain. Dry and warm, they ripened and sweetened, being removed a small quantity at a time as needed. The ones left in the ground over winter, called stand-overs, turned pithy and unfit to eat. Their vines were cut into short lengths containing four or five buds, then pushed into the bed with a stick with a V notch in the end. The ground was plowed and then hoed into ridges a foot or two high.

The pieces of vine were pushed into the top of the long ridges. The rain water collected in the trenches between the ridges and soaked into the ground. The tubers developed in the ridges, and digging them leveled the ground again. The potatoes were dug with a 5-tined rake shaped like a hoe, called a potato rake. After improved varieties had been developed, one farmer told me that when the ground had been well cow-penned he got four hundred bushels to the acre. At a dollar a bushel that was not a bad return.

Tomatoes were little pear shaped ones about as big as the end of a man's thumb, bright red, seedy and juicy. Ma made catsup of them, using vinegar of her own making from syrup and water. She sealed the bottles with a wax made from beeswax and resin from the pine trees, and squares of clean cloth. A glass bottle filled with small hot peppers, picked at varying stages of development from green though red, covered with vinegar, was a pretty fixture on every dining table. Soda crackers had come in barrels that were left uncovered so customers could help themselves. We always considered it a treat when Pa brought us some from Tampa. Farmers coming to town to trade thought a pound of crackers and a can of sardines for their midday meal made it a feast.

Cakes were made with syrup instead of sugar. Raisins were in clusters on the stem, and along with nuts were kept for a treat on special occasions. Spices could be bought in the stores in Tampa. Col man's dry mustard came in the same little square-cornered yellow tin boxes. Mixed in a cup, about one spoonful of mustard to three of flour, with a few grains of sugar and a few drops of vinegar added, with boiling water to make the spread as thick or thin as desired, it made a nice hot condiment.

Nutmegs were whole, and were grated as needed. Cinnamon came in sticks, and had to be crushed as fine as possible. Cloves were whole. They and black pepper (separately of course) were ground in the coffee mill set as fine as possible. Then the mill had to be thoroughly washed before being used to grind coffee again. Coffee was weighed out by the grocer. It was my job to roast it. How I loved the aroma. After we came to Tampa we could get it already put up in paper bags, roasted. Coffee was made in big tin pots, put in half a cupful or so at a time and water added and boiled over and over till the pot was half full of grounds. The brew was bitter and potent, and drunk by young and old alike, even babies being given an occasional sip. Pure coffee was not liked as well as that adulterated by chicory.

Tea was scarce and high priced and hoarded carefully. One lady from Pennsylvania had a headache one day and gave her landlady her treasured bag of tea to make her a cup of tea. After about two hours, the landlady, deeply distressed, said, "I've boiled it and boiled it, but it just won't get tender." Coca Cola's curious ornate C's greeted one from every billboard and wall. It was served at fountains, not in bottles, five cents for a big glassful.

As the railroads were extended, and sawmills and turpentine stills and phosphate mines had their own commissaries, it became easier for people to get groceries and other items without having to depend on their own ingenuity and skill and hard work. Canned meats, fruits and vegetables did away with annual "starvation time" when the rains and hot sun make okra and eggplant about the only vegetables tough enough to grow, and then only if they had grown big enough to make shade for their own roots before the sun got too hot. Borden's Eagle Brand condensed milk was soon followed by other brands of sweetened milk. Evaporated milk was not far behind. Butter, rank with preservative, came in tin cans. In warm weather it had to be dipped with a spoon. Oleo was equally rank and soft, and for many, many years had to be colored in the home kitchen.

Increased trade meant increased need for money, hitherto nonexistent. Trade was carried on largely by barter. Neighbors exchanged services. Paper bills were in circulation, in the present denominations plus a dollar one. The common coins were silver dollars, halves, quarters, dimes, nickels and pennies. Half-dimes were silver, and tiny. The last time I ever saw one was in 1895. Two-cent coins were copper, but heavy. The last one I saw was in 1889. Gold coins were never in general use.

When we had first pulled into Lakeland some little Negro boys were sitting on the steps of the store across the street from the station, blissfully chewing about the first cane of the season. Ma exclaimed, "Oh, those poor children! So hungry they are eating cornstalks!" It wasn't long before she learned the delight of chewing cane. Most farmers raised all they wanted to chew and make syrup and sugar for their own use. A good syrup maker was sure of sale for all his surplus. It brought a good price, ten cents per quart bottle.

Cane grinding and syrup boiling was always a time for neighborhood gatherings, and wound up with a taffy pull. Rose's husband, Rodolphus Trapnell, was a famous syrup maker. My children looked forward to going out there at cane grinding time, and had a wonderful outing.

Many mills were used by several different families in a community. The cane was cut and the leaves trimmed off in the field. Then it was piled to the side of the one who fed it into the mill. Care had to be exercised to keep the cane fed in at the right time to keep a steady pull on the mill. If the mill was allowed to get empty the whiffletree fell on the horse's heels and the frightened animal broke into a run. The juice was strained through a crocus sack over a barrel. The impurities that rose during the boiling were skimmed off. The boiling juice had to be dipped up with a longhandled dipper and poured back, to keep it from boiling over. If it was stirred, it went to sugar. Bees that were attracted by the aroma and overcome by the heat and fell in were promptly scooped out. The kettle was a big shallow one holding forty to sixty gallons. It was set in a fireplace made of clay, with a firebox big enough to take cordwood. The chimney was eight to ten feet high, enough to reach a couple of feet above the roof of the open shed in which the fireplace stood. It took about four hours to boil a kettleful of juice into syrup. When the syrup was the right consistency, it took fast action to dip it into barrels, and to throw in a bucketful of fresh juice to keep the syrup on the bottom of the kettle from burning. It was considered an honor and mark of confidence to be allowed to tend the kettle.

On November 17, 1901, came a freeze that killed all the cane in the county, so there was not enough to make plantings for the next crop. It was while I was teaching my first term of school, and boarding with the W. B. Moodys. A misting rain began shortly after noon. When I got home, Mr. Moody and their older son, Omer, were cutting cane and throwing it in piles and covering it with dirt. He saved enough to make plants for the next year. What he could not cut before dark was frozen. Then, for ten days, they started the kettle at four o'clock in the morning and kept it going till ten at night. A neighbor man came to help. His daughter came to take care of the eight months old baby so Mrs. Moody could work with the syrup making, I washed the breakfast and supper dishes and fed the mill for an hour each afternoon, and cut the noon recess to half an hour, so Omer and Sanford could get home half an hour earlier. Altogether, it was a wonderful example of cooperative effort that got all the cane made up before any of it turned sour.

To celebrate the finishing of the job at noon on Thanksgiving Day, Mr. Moody let me and the teacher of the next nearest school, Elsie Dickinson, go horseback riding. We went out for a mile or so, then turned around to come home. Elsie said, when we came to a patch of heavy sand that we thought would discourage any temptation to run, "Let's lope a little." At the first jump, Elsie's saddle turned and deposited her in the deep sand. Well trained cowponies, both horses stopped in their tracks. Elsie was on her feet by the time I got to her. I cinched the saddle again, as Mr. Moody had taught me to do, and we continued on our way—at a sedate walk.

Oranges were eaten fresh, usually by peeling off enough yellow skin to avoid getting oil on the lips, then cutting a small round hole in the blossom end with a jackknife, the cells punctured by stabbing with the knife and then sucking the juice out. Then the fruit was torn open and the remaining pulp and membrane eaten. Dietetic scientists are telling us now to get the full benefit of the orange the pulp and membrane should be eaten as well as the juice drunk. We ate 'em just because we liked 'em and wanted to get every good mouthful we could.

The first attempts at preserving them in any way was to make wine. Pa brought home a little bottle someone had given him to try. I held the teaspoonful he gave me in my mouth till I could get across the porch and spit it out. They tried making preserves out of peeled skins cut in halves, parboiling them in two or three waters before cooking in syrup. It was eatable, but not worth a second try, not like the delicious orange and grapefruit products we now have.

The temptation to steal was removed by the custom of allowing travelers to climb the fence, take whatever oranges or cane they wanted to eat and could collect in time to run and catch up with the horse that had gone on down the road. If there was too much travel for the farmer's generosity, he simply planted his cane patch farther from the road. The grove couldn't be moved, so he endured the loss without complaint or built a higher fence. Watermelons were always planted too far away to be tempting. They were large and luscious. Boys went out as soon as it was light enough to see in the morning and gathered them while they were cool with dew, and put them in a tub of water, with a cloth over them to keep them cool by evaporation util used. The rinds were pickled or preserved.

Wild persimmons were not very common. Three large trees stood on the east side of Garrett's pond, right in our path to school. The under-ripe ones puckered your mouth like alum. Fully ripe ones were sweet and delicous as the Japanese persimmons, which were not extensively cultivated.

Haws were an ornamental tree with small yellow berries with a thin covering of tasty flesh over brown seeds, a good bit like loquats. Grandma Trapnell said of them, "You can eat them things until you get plum hongry."

Mulberries were planted principally for their shade. People wouldn't eat the berries because of the tiny bugs crawling over them, not realizing that they were fertilizing the bloom. Children loved them and ate them regardless of the bugs. There were many mulberry trees on the streets of Tampa, making highly desirable shade in summer, shedding their leaves in winter. One was on the corner of Franklin and Twiggs Streets, for a good many years after the Gulf National Bank, the predecessor of the Exchange National Bank, was built in 1894, where people could tie their horses in the shade while they attended to business.

Emma N. Gaylord and her children, seated (L to R) Dorothy Beatrice and Stanley. Standing: Herbert, Frank and Nathalie, Sept. 15, 1918.

Emma Nancy Dreyer, Christmas, 1901.

Sept., 1886, bottom row (L. to R.): Mary Elida Dryer, age 10, Emma Nancy Dreyer, age 5. Seated: Caroline Bennett Zerau, 43, Nancy Cabelia Dreyer, 45, Julia Ann Cole, 21, on her lap, William Wesley Cole, 1. Back row: William Zerau, 41, John Zerau, 17, Minnie Louise Dreyer, 17, Rose Lorraine Dreyer, 12, Wesley Cole, 25.

EAGLE BRAND
ROOT BEER!
HIRES' IMPROVED
Saved by Acme Soap.
ONE APPLICATION GIVES RELIEF
FOR PILES
SAMPLE FREE
Witch Hazel Oil

Dinky Line, the F. B. Knowles in the yard at Orlando.

Cloverleaf Hall

Rollins College

Old Horseshoe, Knowles Hall (burned Dec. 2, 1909), Pinehurst, Dining Hall.

Blackberries as big as a man's thumb grew in profusion on old mill sites or other places where there was an abundance of rotting wood. Alas, such patches were the haunt of redbugs and rattlesnakes. Huckleberries and blueberries were abundant, but there were no wild strawberries.

Cultivated grapes were not successful. The bronze skinned scuppernong was found at almost every house, growing with practically no cultivation, bearing in clusters of three or four berries. Eaten raw, the taste was good. The skins were so tough no effort was made to make jam or jelly. Wild grapes grew in abundance in swamps. They were an accurate weather prognosticator. When they put out their leaves all danger of cold was over. They were so sour no one wanted to eat them. Sugar was too scarce and high priced to make jelly.

Peaches did not do well. The only variety, found one or two trees at each home, was a small, round, flat clingstone, called "pinto." I judge it a Spanish importation.

Only one variety of pear grew here, a hard, grainy, juiceless one unfit for eating raw, but delicious when cooked, especially if a tiny bit of lemon peel was added.

Wild plum trees were beautiful in the spring when covered with white bloom. The fruit was so sour it was left for the hogs, so they were called hog plums. Later, about the time of World War I, it was learned how a delicious jelly could be made.

Tropical fruits such as avocadoes, mangoes, papayas, bananas and guavas would grow here. They were too susceptible to cold to be raised extensively. The same was true of pineapples. Guavas grow wild in the tropics the world around, and in Florida south of Fort Myers. Hogs eat them eagerly. Many people refuse even to taste them, though they are nourishing and rich in Vitamin C. Many are the jokes told about their smell, which is a delightful aroma or a horrible stench, depending on the individual's point of view. In the summer of 1894 I canned and sent Mary a two-quart jar of them, which she served for her wedding dinner. When asked how he liked them, the minister replied tactfully, "Very well; but I can't imagine myself hankering for them."

Flour came in one hundred ninety-six pound barrels, or in half barrels. If a smaller quantity was wanted, it was weighed out by the grocer in a paper sack. Not for a good many years was it put in sacks at the mill. It was only about the time we came to Florida that what was known as the "roller process" of milling flour or oatmeal was invented.

Grits was a staple made of white corn that took the place of rice and Irish potato, and was served for virtually every meal. Those who liked coarse grits said they didn't want cornmeal, while those who preferred fine ones proclaimed they didn't want hominy.

Until after World War I it was customary for the grocery stores to send out a man with horse and buckboard to make the rounds of their regular customers to take orders. Self-service stores came into being about the close of the war. The driver dropped to the ground a "hitching block" attached to the end of the reins, a cast iron disk about six inches across by two deep, and the horse stood still. If kerosene was needed, the can could be taken to the store. The same could be done with the syrup jug. Those living reasonably close to the store got delivery the same day, those farther away the next. After telephones became commoner, a woman could call in an order and have it in an hour. There were no child labor laws then, so there were plenty of jobs for young boys, both with and without bicycles, to deliver groceries.

The practice gave plenty of opportunity for cheating. Many a pound of sugar weighed fourteen ounces. Many a pound of meat contained an ounce or two of wrapping paper. Vinegar and milk were the same price, ten cents a quart. One girl whose father ran a dairy told her grocer sternly, "When we sell a quart of milk, we have to fill the bottle full; now you fill my bottle with vinegar." Sales tickets were made out as purchases were ordered.

Chickens were scrawny mongrels. They roosted in trees or on joists in sheds, or, rarely, in a coop. We could get oats in Tampa, and bran to make mash to supplement the usual corn. They could catch enough bugs and worms to provide their own protein. Grit was lacking. It was my job to pound broken dishes with a hammer on a board to pieces small enough for a hen to swallow. Oyster shells were broken the same way. Eggs were few, and ranged in price from twenty cents a dozen in early spring to forty cents around Christmas, when folks wanted them for cakes and eggnog.

Game was abundant. Fryers sold for fifteen cents apiece, live. When beef was wanted, neighbors shared the labor of butchering, each taking a portion of the meat and taking turns in furnishing the animal. Each family was usually big enough to consume a hog. They went out in the woods with dogs and caught one or more. What they could not eat fresh they cured in their log smokehouses, using corncobs or hickory chips. All bones had to be removed from hams and shoulders. The product was dark colored and dry, but delicious when boiled with vegetables.

A man used to come around occasionally with fresh pork and beef. In Tampa there were regular butchershops with refrigerators of artificial ice. In them one could buy the best from Chicago, slaughtered by such packers as Armour and Swift, shipped in cars refrigerated by natural ice. By that time John Long had built a factory on the river below LaFayette Street. He sold ice for ten cents a hundred pounds delivered. Some few householders had factory made refrigerators. More had homemade iceboxes, inefficient and wasteful, but a big improvement over a pan of water on the shelf on a porch on which a dish of food could be placed, covered with a cloth wet and cooled by evaporation.

CHAPTER VI

WHAT WE LIVED BY

In virtually every house there was at least one person who could read the Bible aloud to the family. Baptist and Methodist papers were carefully read. Church buildings were few. Services, including Sunday school, were held in schoolhouses and homes. For the rare night meetings, people brought their own lamps and lanterns. After one such service I remember seeing one man lay his sleeping four-year-old son across his shoulder and start leading his family on the three-mile walk home through the woods by the light of the stars. To me it was indicative of the deep desire of his heart for the Word and worship of God. Circuit riders made regular rounds.

Fifth Sunday services brought worshipers for miles in every direction, on foot, on horseback, in buggies and ox wagons. One backless seat in the wagon held the driver and two others. The rest were seated in chairs or on the floor of the wagon bed. Oxen traveled about four miles an hour, horses not much faster. The morning sermon was at least an hour long. Each family brought dinner, which was spread on tables or on the ground under the shady oaks. Some of the men ate with their razor sharp jackknives. The afternoon service was as long as the morning one. I do not suppose any of those early preachers could be considered educated. But they were dedicated men whom God used to present His Word and give guidance and instruction in righteousness.

After the afternoon service people went home in time to do their evening chores. They had not only feasted on the Word of God and the best food the women knew how to prepare, but had also met friends and heard the news for miles around.

For many years itinerant teachers went about holding singing schools that lasted for two or three weeks. They were good teachers and the folks apt pupils. In every community there was at least one man who could pick up a hymnbook, open it at random, read the music, familiar or unfamiliar, and lead the congregation in singing. There were many good singers. Of some it could only be said they made a joyful noise. But all sang, psalms and hymns and spiritual songs, making melody unto the Lord in their hearts.

Every year in October the Methodists held a camp meeting at Pleasant Grove. They had eloquent preachers, sound Bible expositors, and good singers, who taught them many of the gospel hymns that are now sung the world around.

Most boys and some girls could play the mouthorgan. A good many folks had violins, which they played largely by ear. Fiddlers were looked upon with scorn by most of their neighbors, who regarded them as idle ne'er-do-wells. But it was fine for a girl to have an organ and lessons to learn to play it. They were handled by agents in the same way as sewing machines. Their homes became the gathering place for young folks in the evenings, especially Sunday evening, where they sang to their heart's content. They usually sang the hymns they knew.

Good music teachers lived in almost every community. Bessie Bryant, about the first one to get an organ, rode horseback eight miles each way to take an hour lesson once a week.

The first pianos were brought by people from the North by the railroad. They were big square or triangular grands. Uprights were invented about the time we came here. Gus Petty opened the first music store in Tampa. His brother-in-law, C. E. Wade, was a piano tuner who lived in Orlando. His sticker is on my piano, which belonged to a lady living in Bartow when it was placed there. A brass plate on the pedal bears the legend, Patented 1893. The serial number shows it to be older than that, dating somewhere between 1885 and 1890.

Quill pens were superseded by steel ones some time between Abraham Lincoln's day and my earliest recollection. Penholders, or penstaffs as they were called here, were of wood, and of various sizes and shapes to suit individual tastes. Every school child for ordinary use had a slate and slate pencil, with a little rag that was wet to clean the slate. I used the slate that had been used by all the older girls in our family, which had been made by Ma's father for Aunt Carrie when she was a girl.

For special training in writing every child above the first grade had a ruled copybook in which he wrote with pen and ink. Many good maxims were thus painstakingly copied. He had a bottle of ink on his desk; the stopper was cork, and liable to produce a spill in the process of removal.

Some desks had little inkwells in them; but the ink evaporated fast. It wrote black and soon faded to brown and on to an almost invisible yellow. There was the same indelible India ink as now. Writing fluid that wrote blue and turned a permanent black was a wonderful improvement. Fountain pens were highly prized by the few who could afford them.

Paper was still made from rags. Linen made the best quality. Wood pulp was not extensively used until about the turn of the century.

In the summer of 1889 Pa told us about a typewriter he had just seen at a neighbor's. I never saw or touched one until I went to the Tampa Business College in 1896. They had a couple of old Remingtons. When Walter Crum announced proudly he had written a whole line in one minute, the rest of us were skeptical. The Remington was a big improvement on earlier machines. The first Smith Premier, with both lower and upper case keys, each character on a separate key, in my opinion has never had a superior for durability and ease of operation. Until about 1900 all makes were what was called "blind." which had to be lifted and tipped back to see what had been written.

Carbon paper had not been invented. Ribbons were of two kinds, black record for writing one copy at a time, and copying, made with a special ink that had a special affinity for soiling fingers. Letters were copied in a book of very thin paper, laid typed side next to the paper, a damp cloth laid over the unprinted side, the next letter laid unprinted side next to the cloth, a book sheet over it, the process repeated until all letters were in place, then the book put in a press with a screw, like an early printing press. It was a messy, tricky operation, the resulting copy frequently blurred and the letter itself showing its wetting.

Erasers were a small knife with a bulge on one side of the point, that had to be used with restraint or a hole was scraped clear through the paper. Paper clips had been invented, but straight pins were the common means of fastening papers together. For legal documents there was a stapler made of cast iron that took an eyelet, which was pressed down by a handle. It made a neat, secure fastening that could not be removed without mutilating the paper. It wasn't beyond a tricky lawyer to remove a sheet and replace it with one more to his notion. So one of the first things Joe Lunsford taught me was never to end a page with the end of a sentence, and especially not the end of a paragraph, but always to carry at least one word onto the next page. Notary's seals were also of cast iron, pressed with a lever, but were movable.

All bookkeeping and other office entries were in longhand. All legal documents were either written out, or printed and the blanks filled in, and copied into the official record books by hand. After typewriters were in most offices, and still blind, most documents for filling out were printed without regard to the space between the lines. No two makes of machine had the same space between lines. So the poor typist had to lift up the platen and adjust the space at the beginning of every line. Very few women were employed in offices then. Miss Julia Ward, the aunt of the president of Rollins College, was at least partly responsible for the introduction of touch typing. She was a teacher at the Perkins Institute for the Blind in Boston, blind herself. The letters she wrote Dr. Ward were very uneven in the pressure of the keys, otherwise just like the work of a seeing person. I had been taught to use three fingers of each hand, spacing with the thumb of the right hand. In a year or two the schools were teaching touch operation.

In 1883 the United States adopted our present standard time. It was made necessary by transcontinental trains and was called railroad time. Country folks continued to set their clocks by the sun. They said so many "hours by sun," and could estimate the time with uncanny accuracy.

Mail came to Seffner daily by train, and from there was sent by horse and buggy to Thonotosassa. The day she expected a letter from "back home" Ma sent me to get it. I loved to go. The pine straw covering the road was soft and smooth to my bare feet, the soughing of the wind in the tops of the pine trees was music to my ears. Clouds passing over the sun made beautiful pictures of light and shade.

Even before the inauguration of rural free delivery, mail was taken one, two, or three times a week by a regular horse and buggy service from a post office at a railway station to one from ten to fifteen miles away, where people living from close by to five or more miles away could go to get it. The biggest change was the difference in parcel post rates, from prohibitive to useable.

New York and Chicago papers reached the stands three or four days late, Jacksonville papers the next day. Many subscribed to the weekly ATLANTA CONSTITUTION.

Daguerrotypes were already obsolete. Tintypes had pretty well run their course. Present day photography had come into being. People said wistfully, if only they could be taken in color. It was still necessary to keep rigid while the picture was being taken. Flashlights had been invented, so pictures could be taken indoors and on dark days. Kodaks were invented about 1897. By that time there were a good many young folks who had money to own and operate one, which they took great pleasure in doing. I have some snapshots taken in 1898, faded and none too good in the first place, but they bring vivid memories of good times. Itinerant photographers went around taking pictures, enlarging them and old ones, tinting them artistically.

Moving pictures reached Tampa about 1897. They were shown on sheets hung on buildings, while the crowds stood in the street to watch. One night Uncle Trapnell and Rose took Virl and Viva to Ybor City. They came back too excited to talk, almost. Under Rose's prompting, Virl could tell about the man pulling off his coat and laying it on a bench. I saw my first one in 1899, while they were still being shown on a sheet outdoors.

Phonographs came along about the same time. They had the long cylinder and big horn of the familiar trademark of the RCA Victor, but without the dog to listen to his master's voice. The first one I saw was owned by a man in Winter Park, who gave a concert by it in Lyman Gymnasium, for which he charged five cents admission. The next summer Dr. David E. Saxton had one. It added to the attraction of two beautiful daughters to bring plenty of young people of both sexes to his home of an evening.

It was a time of epochal inventions and discoveries. Prof. Graham announced to us high school students in the winter of 1895-96 the discovery of X-rays, then called Roentgen rays, from their discoverer.

Automobiles had been invented. As we young folks rode along in our ox wagon we joked about our "horseless carriage." You stepped on the hub and the rim of the wheel and the edge of the wagon bed and down into it, a feat somewhat difficult to perform with ladylike decorum, with our full skirts reaching to our ankles. For older and less agile folks, the tailgate was removed and a chair placed so one could step onto the chair and into the wagon. Then the chair was lifted into the wagon to make a seat. A few had big umbrellas about the size of a small beach umbrella, usually of white canvas that soon became a dirty mildewed gray. Sometimes the seat was a board laid across the top of the wagon bed. The seats were backless, the wagons springless, the roads either heavy sand or so full of pine and palmetto roots we bounced up and down hard enough to jolt your eyeteeth loose; but we rode along, sweltering or in frozen misery according to the weather. Our discomforts did not keep us from enjoying good times, in anticipation, in realization, and in retrospection.

When automobiles came along, their running boards, low enough to step up on easily, were wonderful for pet dogs to ride on, leaning over against the body. Boys likewise. It was safe enough if they held on tight, for the top speed was only about twenty-five miles an hour.

I saw my first auto in the summer of 1900. Walking home from church, at the corner of Henderson and Florida Avenues, we heard a terrific chug-chugging down the street, and watched in fascination as Mr. N. D. Smith came up Florida Avenue, hands gripping the wheel, arms straight out, eyes turning neither to right nor left; a proud and happy man, the first one in Tampa to have one of the new conveyances. Another early owner was Shade Mobley. When he sold the horse and took the car home, his wife said tearfully, "But you can't **love** a thing like that!"

My first ride in an automobile was taken because ordinary politeness wouldn't let me refuse. It was about three blocks long. I held onto the seat for dear life, and was never more thankful than when I could step onto the ground again.

The first bicycles were those monstrosities with high front wheels and tiny back ones. By the time I went to Rollins in 1897, safety bicycles had been invented, both wheels the same size, made for both men and women. Men wore a spring clamp around their right ankle to keep their trousers leg from catching in the chain. Women wore specially made divided skirts that hung down gracefully and modestly to their shoetops.

Bicycles were the first transportation medium to be equipped with pneumatic tires. They came with a little tool box containing among other things a pump for refilling the tire tubes with air. The first attempt at improvement of roads in Hillsborough County was in 1901 by a $400,000 bond issue. The first paved road followed the route of the old sand road from Tampa to Plant City. It was constructed of local limestone, so soft the steel-rimmed wagon wheels riddled it with potholes and ground it to powder, so that in less than two years it was utterly worthless. An unpublished—and unpublicized—itemized statement that I typed showed a cost of more than $10,000 a mile, including the salary of an armed guard for the convict labor used.

The next step was the use of glazed red paving brick imported from Georgia, to make roads the public called "rubber band roads," only wide enough for one car. Vehicles had to pass with the outside wheels off the pavement.

CHAPTER VII

SICKNESS AND HEALTH

Doctors were few and far between. All were busy, none wealthy. Too much of their pay was in the form of a bushel of sweet potatoes for fifty cents, or a day's labor in house or yard in lieu of the same amount. One quite eminent one told me, "What we don't know would make a much larger volume than what we do." But they used the considerable knowledge and skill they did have for the benefit of their fellowmen, not sparing themselves.

Every home had its little stock of medicine. Usually it contained calomel, castor oil, quinine for chills and fever, Cloverine salve (a good one), spirits of turpentine, camphor gum cut in whiskey, and always a small bottle of whiskey. As it was the only pain reliever they had, it was used for a wide variety of ailments. Only in Christmas eggnog was it used as a beverage. Raw rosin pulled from the pine trees was chewed like gum when turpentine was needed for internal medicine.

Dentists were even scarcer than doctors. Their equipment was primitive. Drills were turned by foot treadle. Cocaine was the only pain killer. Gold was the only filling material. Teeth were exceedingly poor. The first teeth were rotted to the gum before the child was old enough for the permanent teeth to come. It was thought the acid in the oranges was responsible for the early decay. It is known now that it was lack of necessary minerals in the soil, and that oranges were a saving influence.

Although tobacco was not grown here, its use was well-high universal. The men carried a plug in their pants pocket, and cut off a small mouthful whenever they wanted it. The women used snuff. To them a "toothbrush" was a small twig two or three inches long, chewed at the soft end until only fibers remained. With that they dipped snuff and placed it behind the lower lip, where it stayed for hours. Many, both men and women, smoked corncob pipes. Some few had factory made pipes. One who wanted to show off might have a Meerschaum. After cigar factories were started here in 1888, more and more smoked the locally handmade Havana cigars.

A chewed twig was also used as a toothbrush. It got teeth clean better than a rag. Toothbrushes, of hog bristles could be bought in Tampa. For dentifrices there were Dr. Lyons Tooth Powder, and a liquid called Rubifoam, which was probably only a red-colored peroxide of hydrogen. Or you could mix salt and soda in your own kitchen and get a product that was effective and nasty as all get out! Salt wet in lemon juice really cleaned the teeth. So did powdered charcoal sifted through a fine cloth.

Very few ever bothered to take any care of their teeth. Walking the floor with a toothache was a common experience. After dentists were available, those who could afford them acquired false teeth. Pride kept them in seclusion till the gums hardened enough for the plates. Well fitting ones were rare.

There were no hospitals. Nursing was done at home by whoever was not too sick himself to do it. I have heard that during the yellow fever epidemics there was frequently no one in the family well enough to take care of the sick. My sister Minnie's husband, John Clifford Sayre, was one of a group of young men who went from house to house just before dark to find out what help might be needed through the night. As always, neighbors came to the rescue. Mrs. Abner Powell, who was Agnes Bourquardez, told me the body of one of her brothers was taken out the kitchen door so another brother would not know he was dead. Many, many families lost more than one member.

So many died that a new cemetery was opened, Woodlawn, some distance north of town. The first person buried there was the wife of the Congregational minister, Rev. Sydney Crawford. My father was the thirteenth or fourteenth person buried there. It was fenced with three strands of barbed wire. One day as Ma was coming back from caring for Pa's grave, she saw a five-foot rattlesnake crawling through the fence and cut off its head with her hoe, not a hundred yards from where she had been working.

Later, both white and colored nurses could be had for a dollar a day, twenty-four hour duty. They not only took care of the sick one, but if it was a mother who was sick, they cooked and washed and ironed and got up at night with any child who might need attention.

Homes were more the center of life then than now. Babies were born there, attended by a doctor or more usually by a white or colored midwife. Most of them were as competent as most of the doctors. Again, neighbors helped. There was generally some near kinswoman to come and take charge of the family until the mother was able to take over again. The maternity death rate was something like one out of sixteen. One infant out of four died before reaching five years of age.

Most weddings were at home or in a church. Funerals were also conducted there. The corpse was laid out by friends and neighbors. Funeral parlors came much later. There were few undertakers in the larger towns. There was a large black hearse drawn by black horses for adults, a much smaller white one drawn by white horses for babies and children not full grown. But until long after we came here the coffin was made by a carpenter and taken to the cemetery in a farm wagon. The procession, short or long, went to the cemetery at a walk, though they generally went away at a trot. No one left until the grave had been filled and mounded up.

I do not remember that I shed any tears at my father's grave—I have never been demonstrative—but I cannot forget how my heart was torn and how I thought if the men only had placed the first shoveful on the box gently instead of throwing it in as they would on an animal, and acted as though they were at least a little bit sorry it had to be done. I think the most poignant remark I ever heard was made many years later. As we stood by the graveside of a mutual acquaintance, a newcomer from Tennessee said to me: "I don't want to be buried here in this sand; I want them to take me back home where there is nice clay." How desperately homesick she must have been.

As sanitation of any sort was lacking, all sorts of filth diseases were rampant: malaria, hookworm (or grounditch as it was then called), diarrhea, dysentery, yellow jaundice, typhoid and yellow fever. Havana was a hotbed of endemic yellow fever. An epidemic of it broke out in Tampa in 1887 and again in 1888. I can remember seeing letters perforated to let fumigation get inside the envelope. People learned they could come to Tampa during broad daylight safely, so they came to a short distance out of town, camped over night, attended to business, and got out again before sundown. When Rose went to Tarpon Springs to teach her first term of school in 1888, they went clear around the head of Old Tampa Bay instead of the more direct route through Tampa, an additional twenty-five miles or so. The old isolation hospital was still standing in old Fort Brooke, south of the city limits, then Whiting Street, when we came here. It was a beautiful spot, much used for picnics.

What little bathing and swimming was done by Tampans was on the white beach at the foot of Franklin Street. It was also the favorite place for baptisms. Rose was baptized there December 8, 1889, becoming a member of the First Baptist Church of Tampa. I stood beside Pa during the ceremony, holding his hand. It was the last time I went anywhere with him or held his hand. An epidemic of la grippe, shortened and Anglicized to the grip, was sweeping the country. Pa had contracted it, and went to bed with his last illness the next day, dying January 10, 1890, leaving us the good name that is rather to be chosen than great riches.

The cesspool of iniquity that later was known as Fort Brooke was on the eastern edge of the reservation, separated from the part known as the Garrison by an extensive salt marsh. The Garrison was a beautiful spot, covered with giant live oaks. It had been abandoned by the United States as a military post. The only sign of its occupation was the one story barracks used as an isolation hospital in the yellow fever epidemics. Many families moved in and built their homes. After much litigation, they were finally given "squatters' rights." The marsh was filled in with sand from excavation of the channel in the estuary, and all that area is now given to commerce.

Yellow fever scares occurred every summer. At the first alarm, everybody who could get out of Tampa did so. Those who could afford it went to Atlanta and Asheville. The last scare we had was in 1900. Dr. Hiram Hampton sent Ma and Alice (my niece) to stay with Rose at Hopewell. He told me, "If I were as young and slender as you are, I would rather take my chances of having it, for then you would not need to fear it any more." So I stayed. I was working for the real estate firm of Beckwith & Henderson. Mr. W. B. Henderson was then the president of the State Board of Health One afternoon just before closing time a man came into his office so excited he could scarcely talk enough to ask if we were going to have yellow fever. Mr. Henderson leaned back in his swivel chair and said calmly, "Yes, we're going to have it, and we're going to have it bad; and if you take it, inside of a week you'll be either an immune or an angel." The man laughed and went out quietly, his panic dissipated. We did not have any yellow fever.

The last smallpox epidemic was in the fall of 1905, lasting two or three months. By that time vaccination had begun to have its effect. Of five hundred very mild cases, only one died. He was an old fisherman living alone in a dirty hovel on Shell Point, below Ballast Point. My husband contracted it while wiring for the Florida State Fair, and broke out Thanksgiving Day. He was taken to the isolation hospital at Buffalo Avenue and the river the following Monday, and got back home the day before Christmas. Mrs. Walters, who lived in the house with us, refused to be vaccinated. They vaccinated me, although it had been only six years since I had been vaccinated. When it didn't take, the authorities were sure I had already contracted it, and for the next few weeks they kept me under constant watchcare.

A peaceful, uneventful week went by. On Monday neighbors took Mrs. Walters, a newcomer from Montgomery, and her baby for a sightseeing trip to the Tampa Bay Hotel. It was very cold, with a high wind blowing, and they kept commenting on how nice and warm little Elizabeth was keeping. That night Mrs. Walters began burning with fever so high she was delirious. Thursday Elizabeth broke out, the morning she was five weeks old, the youngest smallpox patient on record. Saturday afternoon they took Mrs. Walters to the isolation hospital although she was free of fever, because they could not take Elizabeth without her. Sunday morning she broke out. The same morning my first baby, Frank, was born. When the doctors were worried about my being alone with only a colored woman to take care of me, I told them I was better protected by the smallpox sign on the door than if I had a cordon of police around me.

My husband and Mrs. Walters had no scars at all. Elizabeth had one tiny one on the end of her little nose. Only those who have seen the horrible scars of smallpox can have any idea how marvelous that was. They were never able to vaccinate Frank until 1966, when he was preparing to go to Iran. That was the last time we had smallpox in Tampa, except an isolated case or two. I have not heard of any for forty years.

When the health authorities took my husband and Mrs. Walters to the pesthouse, they took their mattresses and all the bedding that had been over them. The only blanket left me was one that had been over Elizabeth. A class of little ten or twelve year old girls in the Tampa Heights Methodist Church had made a comforter covered with white cheesecloth as a missionary project. They sent it to me by the man who came to take my grocery order. The memory of their kindness brings a glow to my heart still. I did not know I had so many friends who provided for me so generously in my need. Of course, it goes without saying that not one of them was allowed to come to see me.

When our first child, Franklin Ward, was born there was smallpox in the house. When the next one, Nathalie Ruth, was born, Frank was having whooping cough. I said to the doctor, "What'll it be for the next one?" He replied casually, "Oh measles or mumps." But the younger three, Herbert Russell, Stanley Hampton, and Dorothy Beatrice, arrived without any sort of contagious disease to greet them. Whooping cough came along in due time, to all except Frank and Nathalie, and all had chickenpox and measles. Mumps waited till Beatrice's tenth birthday, January 29th, 1924 when she developed them. The others followed one at a time, till Herbert had them just in time to miss some of his exams at close of school, in June.

The authorities fumigated the whole house with sulphur, except the room I was in. It didn't do any good, but it did ruin the Seth Thomas clock that was one of our wedding presents, and the sewing machine I had rented from the next door neighbor. She accepted five dollars for it, setting the price herself. I shortly thereafter bought the New Home I am still using, paying thirty-five dollars for it, five dollars down and three dollars a month for ten months. It was a treadle machine, light and easy running.

Typhoid fever in 1913, followed by rheumatic fever in 1914, left my heart in such condition I could no longer run it myself. So from then until we got electricity in this area in 1921, the children took turns in getting down in behind the machine and pushing the connecting rod up and down. It was fun until they got tired, then it wasn't funny. They were as thankful as I was when Daddy bought me a Hamilton Beach home motor, which I have never used for any purpose other than the sewing machine. I saved the treadle until the wartime drive for scrap iron was on in 1942.

CHAPTER VIII

PROGRESS AND FREEZES

Tampa was getting to be quite a business center, and was incorporated as a city in 1887. The first bridge, the LaFayette Street, replaced the ferry across the Hillsborough River when Mr. Henry B. Plant began building the Tampa Bay Hotel, and a quicker and more convenient way of getting to it was needed. More people were settling west of the river, too. There was a ferry at the mouth of Six Mile Creek, now Palm River, and one near the mouth of the Alafia River, until after 1900. Fords were the usual crossings of streams. One community had a little ferry across the Alafia at Dees Ford, used only when the flooded river made it needed. It was barely big enough for one wagon and horse or yoke of oxen, unhitched from the wagon, at a time, and was poled across. Mr. Dees kept it on his side of the river. When anyone wanted to come from the other side, he hollered for Mr. Dees to bring it. If a stream was too small to need a ferry, when it was flooded enough to make horses or oxen swim, we put our feet up on the dashboard and went on through.

Sailing vessels were still in common use, though gradually being replaced by steamers. The channel was so narrow, shallow and crooked it was customary for vessels to go aground on Big Island, one of those incorporated in Davis Islands (plural) when they were filled in. Cargo was brought by lighter to the docks on the east side of the river. Sidewheel steamers made regular runs to Manatee River points as far up as Ellenton. Bradenton was then Braidentown. Sarasota was a fishing camp. A small steamer made daily round trips to and from St. Petersburg. (Only folks didn't call it St. Pete in those days; it was the Saintly City.) A favorite recreation in hot weather was a cruise down the bay on moonlight nights.

One lady who lived at Anona said, "In the old days we drove by horse and buggy to Clearwater, took the train to St. Petersburg, then the steamer to Tampa, attended to our business and retraced our journey, and thought we had been somewhere."

Even the fastest trains, such as the FLYING CRACKER of the Florida Central & Peninsular Railroad, which became the Seaboard Air Line, and the CANNON BALL of the South Florida Railroad (later the Plant System, then the Atlantic Coast Line, and now part of the Seaboard Coast Line), were hauled by wood burning engines. The cordwood was stacked on racks alongside the tracks, for easy transfer to the tender. The top speed was about twenty miles an hour. And that is about as far as they could go without taking on more wood. It took an hour to go from Tampa to Plant City, five hours to Winter Park. Pay for the wood, made a nice addition to the cash income of the farmers along the way. In cold weather the coach was heated by a wood stove. In hot weather the passengers endured the heat. If they kept the windows closed, it was hotter. If they opened them, the smoke and cinders poured in. Grime on skin and clothes was inevitable. Coaches were lighted by kerosene lamps hung from the ceiling, that swung back and forth with the motion of the train.

Mr. Henry B. Plant extended his railroad to Port Tampa City, where he located repair shops and turntable. He built a pier a mile long out to water deep enough for ocean going vessels. About three-quarters of the way out he built the PORT TAMPA INN, a small but comfortable hotel. It was a place for passengers to stay overnight while making connections between train and boat. It shortly became a great resort for those who did not want to go out in boats to fish. There was a hole about four feet square cut in the floor of the back porch, where all the kitchen and table scraps were dumped. Fish swarmed to the feasts. A man could fish through the hole or over the porch railing. He could have his catch cooked and served for dinner.

All through trains went clear to the end of the pier, where ocean going vessels could dock. Mail boats went to Havana regularly twice a week, with mail and passengers for Key West and Havana and points beyond.

Local trains were run from Tampa morning and evening. Parties went for swimming as well as fishing. Picnics were held on a small island called Picnic Island.

I have many times mentioned the coming of the railroads as a pivotal event in the development of Florida. I feel that too high tribute cannot be given to the far-sighted men who were willing to venture their money to open up a truly underdeveloped land. When we came to Tampa, from where the railroad crossed Franklin Street bridge where the depot stood, the river swamp growth was cut off in a straight vertical wall by the passage of the Atlantic Coast Line trains. When I think of the tremendous part played by the railroads in bringing prosperity to Florida, I have little patience with those who fret or even rage at the little annoyances caused by having the tracks pass through town. I have always enjoyed watching the freight trains pass, noting the great distances some of the cars were from their home base.

The first time I went through the famed Tampa Bay Hotel, we walked on 2″ x 12″ planks laid across the floor joists. A good many young men served their entire apprenticeship as brickmasons on the one building, which was four years under construction. It was thrilling to climb the spiral stairs and look out the minaret windows on a solid green carpet of treetops. Mr. Plant had spur tracks built clear to the west side of the building, so guests could get in and out of trains under shelter. He had trainload after trainload of sand dumped to fill in the marsh along the river. He brought cabbage palmettoes in on flatcars, and had experts plant them. They are still adorning Plant Park. The hotel opened in January, 1891. I attended the first orchestra concert given in the round music room.

Phosphate was discovered about 1890. Phosphora was the first mine opened. Bone Valley and Prairie Pebble soon followed, then others in rapid succession. It was the biggest boost the economy of Florida ever had. Farmers worked at the mines and continued to till the soil. New settlers meant a market for surplus produce. Railroads reached into hitherto inaccessible areas. The Nichols mine was on the land homesteaded by my brother-in-law's grandfather, a Mr. Miller. He had been a school teacher in Georgia, and brought quite a few families with him, many of them his kindred. Descendants of theirs still live in the area.

The Bell Telephone Company had come to Tampa before we did, and by the summer of 1895 had a 300-connection switchboard. Another company organized an exchange on the West Coast, serving St. Petersburg and Clearwater. The Peninsular Telephone Company was organized, with Mr. W. D. Brorein as its prime mover. It bought as many of the outlying local exchanges as it could, and became so formidable a rival that the Bell Company finally sold to it.

In the summer of 1903 I worked for McNamee & Lunsford, its attorneys. Mr. Brorein dictated a good many letters and other documents to me over the phone, so it was nothing unusual to have him dictate a letter, and following his custom have me read it back to him. It was not till afterward I learned he had been talking from Bradenton, and that that letter was the first message to come over the long distance line from Bradenton.

"Freeze coming!" is a phrase that still strikes dismay to the hearts of all, but none since to quite the extent as did the Big Freeze of February 8, 1895, which proved to be a blessing in a mighty black disguise. Grove owners went to bed wealthy and woke too poor to pay their taxes. Many of them had waited till after the holidays to sell their fruit for better prices. A severe freeze on December 29th had frozen all the fruit on the trees and knocked off all the leaves.

Six weeks of springlike weather with plenty of rain caused new growth to start. It was from ten to eighteen inches long when another cold wave hit, splitting the trees from top to bottom. Weather bureau records show it came the fastest of any on record. Wednesday morning was like May. Friday morning Mr. Thompson woke us by calling, "Wake up, Mrs. Dreyer; it's snowing." Being from snow country, Ma sent me on to school. Out of an enrollment of seventy-five in Hillsborough High, there were fifteen boys and girls present. Prof. Graham told us at morning recess, "Now, boys and girls, I want you to go out and play snowball, for it's probably the only chance you'll ever have." So we scraped up snow that had collected at the cracks of the board sidewalk enough to make balls about the size of golf balls, and threw them at one another. I have seen a little snow in the air a few times since, but never on the ground.

Most of the schools in the state closed immediately. There was no money in the county treasuries and no prospect of being able to collect any. One woman from somewhere in the central part of the state said her school simply gave the boys and girls their diplomas, four months short of the required amount of instruction. Prof. Graham and Mrs. Louisa Tucker Phillips, the only other teacher in Hillsborough High, continued to teach without pay till the end of the full term. Prof. Graham has been honored by having an elementary school named for him, but so far as I know nothing has ever been done to acknowledge the debt of gratitude to Mrs. Phillips. I should like to see a Junior High school named for her, for she taught the ninth and tenth grades for four or five years. She was the first woman to teach in Hillsborough High. She was the daughter of a governor of Bermuda, a musician of high order, a consecrated Christian. She refused the chair of English and history at East Florida Seminary, the predecessor of the University of Florida, to take the work here because she felt this was the needier field.

The blessing part of the freeze was that up to that time people had been depending on their groves for their income. They couldn't live on nothing the four or five years it would take the groves to recover, so they turned to raising vegetables. That was the beginning of our great truck gardening industry. Up till that time there had been no market for any surplus, so farmers raised only enough for their own use. But settlers were coming in like a flood, and markets were further expanded by the invention of refrigerated cars in which fresh fruits and vegetables could be shipped as far as New York and Chicago and arrive in good condition. Strawberries were among the early money-makers. One man near Dover said of raising them, "It's low down, dirty work, but there's money in it, and it's clean money too."

Another big freeze occurred on February 12th or 13, 1899. The old courthouse had been moved to about where Grant's downtown store is now and turned into a rooming house facing Florida Avenue. It burned to the ground that night. It was the only time in the history of the Tampa Fire Department that water froze as it fell from the hoses.

The fire department started as a volunteer organization, and drew into it all the up-and-coming young men of the town. The hose reel was kept in a little square building just big enough for the purpose, facing west on Florida Avenue in the block south of Scott Street, with a little tower beside it where the fire alarm bell hung. Several other towns had similar volunteer departments. Each year they held a competitive exhibition of skill. In 1890 it was held in Tampa, the races being run on LaFayette Street between Ashley Street and Florida Avenue. The whole town turned out to see and cheer.

Next came steam pumps drawn by magnificent horses. The Tampa Heights engine house was where the educational building of the Palm Avenue Baptist church is now. It was next door to Dr. Hiram J. Hampton's office. He took care of the burns the horses had endured without moving out of their tracks. Not all heroes are men or dogs.

The people of Florida in those days took an intense interest in politics. Picnics at which candidates presented their views were attended by people from miles around. I attended one at Dees Ford in 1892. The tariff was a hot issue. In the campaign of 1896 the issue was free silver, "Sixteen to one" being the slogan, and William Jennings Bryan, the Democratic candidate and William McKinley the Republican. Election returns came by telegraph to THE TAMPA JOURNAL, and were projected on a sheet hung on the Almeria Hotel across the street. Every once in a while would appear the statement, "Bill's ahead," followed immediately by the question, "Which Bill?" Uncle Trapnell came home at midnight, the election still undecided.

No stress was laid on size of voting districts, nor how many voters each contained. At least one voting place, at what is now Balm, was a pile of half-dozen or so logs, where the free voters could cast their ballots. Voting machines were invented after women were given the franchise in 1920, no longer classed along with criminals and idiots, unfit to vote. But they exerted a powerful influence on the thinking of their husbands.

Devout Democrats though most of them were, the people truly mourned the tragic death of President McKinley in 1901. To many, Republican was synonymous with Publican.

CHAPTER IX

ROLLINS COLLEGE, 1897

In June of 1896, Mr. Noah D. Smith, who had taken an interest in me after my father died, insisted that I must take a ten-week course at the Tampa Business College. It cost $15.00. He gave us an extension of time for making payments on a lot we were buying from him. I had seven weeks training before a smallpox epidemic closed the school. After Christmas I was offered the position as stenographer by Dr. Ward, the president of Rollins College in Winter Park where I went on January 7, 1897. Monday morning I attacked a three-weeks accumulation of Dr. Ward's letters, taking dictation in short hand and transcribing it in longhand, because I could do nothing with the old Blickensderfer typewriter. Later, we had a succession of very good typewriters.

The present campus of Rollins bears no resemblance to the one I knew. It consisted of twenty acres, fenced on three sides with three strands of barbed wire. Lake Virginia was the southern boundary. The six buildings were located around what was called the Horseshoe: Knowles Hall at the northeast tip, Pinehurst, the dining hall, Lyman Gymnasium, Lakeside and Cloverleaf, on the site of the present library. Knowles Hall, which housed the recitation rooms and the chapel, burned, as did the dininghall. Cloverleaf was moved down by the lake, off from the Horseshoe, to make way for the library. Water oaks, about the nicest shade tree grown in Florida, had been planted around the Horseshoe, and were very, beautiful.

A board sidewalk led between Cloverleaf and the dininghall. The other walks were cinder paths. A board walk connected the front steps of each building to the path around the Horseshoe. The area thus enclosed was supposed to have a lawn. But every year the sandspurs were burned off, which of course only destroyed the good grass and made the sandspurs germinate faster.

Old photographs show the original buildings. But they don't show how superior they were to the homes from which most of the students came. They were comparative palaces. The inside walls were plastered, for one thing.

In a day when few public buildings were heated at all, and most schoolrooms only by a wood heater, Knowles Hall was heated by hot air registers in each classroom, Pinehurst and Lakeside by hot air registers in the first-floor halls, supplemented by a fireplace in the corner of the livingroom on the ground floor. The furnace was in an excavation in the sand under the building, and took wood almost as big as cordwood. The dininghall was heated by a fireplace, toasting those near it while freezing those by the door. But there were not many meals at which the heat was not sufficient for comfort anywhere in the rooms.

Cloverleaf had hot water registers in each bedroom; the halls and parlors no heat at all. In a cold wave the boiler, in a little building between the southeast and west wings, was started, but by the time the registers were hot enough to affect the temperature the cold wave was over, and we sweltered until they cooled again. I remember the same cold wave that froze the hose water when the old courthouse burned here in Tampa. We had a Valentine party in the north parlor of Cloverleaf, hung blankets over the arched doorways, brought in oil heaters, kept our coats on, and had a wonderful time.

Pinehurst was the original women's cottage, and Lakeside the men's. By the time I got there in the spring of 1897, Cloverleaf had been built, and Pinehurst taken for offices for Dr. Ward's living quarters, and visitors' room.

The library was in one room on the first floor. I don't suppose there were more than five or six hundred volumes on the shelves. Most of them were old books then, that would be valued now for their age if not for their contents.

The next year I moved to Cloverleaf, and Pinehurst took the overflow from Lakeside. Cloverleaf was so named because of its shape: three wings, southeast, northeast, converged in one big central room surrounded by three smaller ones in a puzzling maze.

As I remember it, there were accommodations for about fifty girls. On the first floor, in the southeast wing, Miss Eva Lamson, the matron, had a sitting room and a bedroom on the corner, with a room with a practice piano on the end towards the front of the building. On the other side, the corner room was another practice room. The front room was my bedroom. In the angle formed by the two wings stood the tiny building housing the boiler that heated the water from a well just outside the building. When the pump and the boiler and the two pianos (one for vocal and the other instrumental) were all going at once—well, learning to shut my ears and pay no attention to extraneous noises was discipline that proved invaluable in later life.

As the demand for water grew greater, a little building was built on the shore of Lake Virginia, and water for every purpose except drinking and cooking pumped from the lake, and the school laundry was moved from under the kitchen to that building. Under the stairs on the first floor in the west wing of Cloverleaf was a sink connected to a septic tank. Over it Billum, the handy man, had put a hand painted sign, FOR WASHING PURPUS ONLY. Under the stairs on the first floor in the southeast wing was a water cooler. The ice was brought from Orlando.

The west wing had four bedrooms on each side. Miss Longwell had two rooms, corresponding to Miss Lamson's. Mrs. Baker had a room on the other side, while Dr. Baker and their son Norman were in Lakeside.

The first and second floors were pretty well filled, but only a few rooms on the third were occupied. They were considered desirable rooms, for they were above the flies and mosquitoes that got in in spite of screens on the windows and doors. On the second floor, over one of the parlors, was a bathroom with three zinc-lined tubs. There was hot water only on Saturdays. On the third floor, which had dormer windows in every room, was a room for storing trunks. Every room had a good-size closet where she could hang clothing.

All three dormitories had rooms built and furnished for a single occupant and most were connected with another. The occupants were called roommates and were allowed to visit one another freely, but had to sleep in their own rooms. Each room had a single bed, a dresser with a mirror, a desk and kerosene lamp, a rocking chair and a straight chair, a light-weight rug, a washstand with plain white bowl and pitcher, and a slop jar. The oak furniture in Cloverleaf was somewhat larger than the walnut in the other two. Each student furnished all the bedding except the counterpane. Each one emptied his own slops out on the ground at Pinehurst and Lakeside. A girl who was working her way emptied them in Cloverleaf; but if the occupant failed to provide sufficient water in the pitcher to rinse the slop jar it didn't get rinsed. Each floor had a sink under the west stairway like the one on the first floor, all connected to the same septic tank.

On each floor was a room where the girls could fill and clean their own lamps and chimneys. Broken chimneys had to be replaced at a cost of ten cents each. Each student took entire care of his or her own room. At Christmas and Easter vacations an army of colored women mopped all floors, washed all windows, and laundered all counterpanes. Some of the girls had lace curtains, bureau scarfs and pictures

There was hot running water in the kitchen, at some three or more sinks, connected to a septic tank near the barn. The laundry where the college washing was done—tablecloths and such things—was in the basement under the kitchen. Flatirons were heated on the wood stove where the clothes were boiled. Students who wanted to were allowed to do their washing and ironing there, furnishing their own soap and starch. At first the college used lye soap made by the cook, and after that, commercial soap. Tablecloths were changed every other day after the midday meal, washed the next day and ironed the next. Each summer Miss Merrill bought a year's supply in the North, beautiful fine linen.

She also bought a year's supply of dishes, good quality plain white chinaware. And plain glasses. Colored girls washed the dishes; girl students who waited on table washed the glasses and silver plated knives and forks.

Some seventy-five or eighty people ate in the dininghall. They were seated eight or ten at a table, each presided over by a member of the faculty or official of some sort. Willard Eliot was head of one, Miss Merrill of another, Dr. Baker of another. We absorbed a lot of culture just through such association with them.

Punctuality was stressed in everything. Miss Merrill stood with her watch in her hand, then buzzed Cloverleaf first, then Lakeside, then Pinehurst. Five minutes was long enough for a girl to come from the farthest reaches of Cloverleaf. After five minutes Miss Merrill locked the door, and any late comer was out of luck till the next meal. Everyone stood behind his chair until the blessing had been asked, by some head of table, then all sat down at the same time, and the din started. No restriction was placed on what we talked about, nor how loudly we spoke. Nor was any restriction placed on how much we ate. But everyone at each table remained seated until the last one was through eating, then at a signal from the head of the table, all rose. All students were required to attend gym unless excused for some good reason. I was too busy with my office work. But from my typewriter I could look out the window and see both boys and girls playing tennis on the clay covered court. The girls wore long white duck skirts and white blouses, the boys ordinary pants, usually also of white duck. For gym the girls wore black sateen bloomers and white shirtwaists. The boys wore the same suits they do now for basketball, short pants and bare knees.

Both boys and girls played basketball. The boys had a baseball team. They played Sanford and Kissimmee that I remember. Those two were close enough by for the teams to make the round trip in one day, by train. At Sanford a wrong decision was made; the Rollins captain, Ralph Evernden, put his bat behind him and sat on it, saying, "This game doesn't go on till that decision is corrected."

The boys could go swimming at the dock on the campus, diving into water six or eight feet deep. Not till after my day were the girls permitted to walk to the west end of the lake, where the water was shallow, before going in.

Mr. Morse was instrumental in getting some canoes given to the college for both boys and girls. One afternoon they were on Lake Maitland near the Seminole Hotel. A twenty-foot alligator had escaped from the pen where the hotel kept him. Edith Foulkes trailed her hand through the water, and pulled it up just barely ahead of Old John's snout. She was still white at supper.

About 1898 the golf course was laid out. Golf was new in Florida. Several of the teachers and students played. Mr. Morse had two loves: his Bible and his golf. After he learned that I could take and transcribe accurately, as soon as he finished his afternoon dictating he went to the course, leaving me to sign and mail the letters.

No memoir of Rollins would be complete without a mention of Old Kate. She may at one time have been pretty, for her coat was still a bright shining sorrel. But a more dejected looking creature could hardly be imagined as she ambled along with her head hanging to her knees, pulling a buckboard as decrepit as herself. The next year there was a big bay, that was said to have been a former circus horse. After that they hired whatever they needed from the local livery stable. When Dr. Ward was there, a horse and buckboard was kept tied to the hitching post by the office. Much of the time the horse was a pretty black one that looked like a Black Hawk.

Ordinarily, a student collected the outgoing mail from all the cottages, and took it to the postoffice. He brought the incoming mail from the postoffice to the head of each cottage, who distributed it to the students. One morning Dr. Ward looked at his watch and exclaimed in dismay, "It's only three minutes till train time, and the boy hasn't come to collect the mail!" I said, "Let me have your horse, and I think we can make it." So Miss Merrill grabbed the letters. We went on around the Horseshoe, across the ball field, through the woods, and pulled up at the depot just in time for Miss Merrill to run and hand the letters to the mail clerk as the train was starting to pull out.

The little horse seemed to sense the urgency, for he went faster than he ever did for Dr. Ward, with no urging except my voice. I still think that half-mile in about five minutes, in heavy sand part of the way, was pretty fast traveling. I let him walk back by the clay-covered road, so he was cooled down by the time we got there.

A few chickens were kept at the barn. One day Mrs. Ward, not much more than a girl herself, city bred, came into the office to show Mr. Ward the day-old chick she had cupped in her hand. The little fellow was yipping his head off. I told her, "Make the sound the old hen makes." She looked at me blankly, and said, "I don't know what that is." I trilled a soothing "Crrrrnk." To her surprise and delight, the baby hushed immediately.

Outside of class and study hours, we were allowed to do just about as we pleased. We could go to town, visit friends among the townspeople, take long walks. It was seven miles around the lake. Mrs. Baker went with me once. A half dozen or so of us walked the four miles out —and four miles back—to Mr. Temple's place to see the bougainvillea plant in his greenhouse, just introduced from Cuba. But no matter where we went or what we did, we had to be in the dininghall at six.

After supper at six and until study began at seven, we could stroll around the campus, sit on benches and talk, (where many a romance started and flourished), or go in the parlor and play games; carroms and parchesi. Boys were allowed on the porch and in the parlors of Cloverleaf. Girls were not allowed in Pinehurst and Lakeside.

At nine-thirty Miss Lamson or her assistant rang a little bell in warning, at ten just a tinkle, and lights had to be out. I was usually sound asleep before that. The big bell in Knowles Hall rang at six-thirty, in plenty of time for us to be ready for breakfast at seven. Sunday morning it rang an hour later, with breakfast at eight. Dinner was at one-thirty instead of twelve, and supper at five-thirty instead of six, to accommodate Sunday school and church goers.

Everyone had to attend chapel at eight-thirty, Monday through Friday. When Dr. Ward was there, he conducted the services: Bible reading, prayer and singing a hymn. At that time at Rollins chapel was held every morning. At its close, two mornings a week Dean E. C. Hills gave us a fifteen minute review of current events. In 1901 he announced the success of Marconi in sending a wireless message in Morse code from Newfoundland to Ireland. Electricity was just beginning its astounding application to virtually every aspect of our lives. One discovery and invention followed another with dizzying rapidity.

In his absence some member of the faculty acted. I remember Prof. Ford, Dr. Baker, and Dean Hills. We had to go to church Sunday morning, taking our choice between Congregational, Methodist, and once a month, Episcopal, the only churches in Winter Park at that time. Attendance at other services was optional. After we had so many Cuban students, a big wagon was hired to take them to the Catholic church in Orlando, to the Sunday morning service only.

The Congregationalists had a flourishing Christian Endeavor Society, the Methodists an equally flourishing Epworth League. Various small groups of students met for prayer meeting. I was one of five or six who met in the room of one of the girls for fifteen minutes after breakfast. Some students, both boys and girls, possibly a half-dozen all told, conducted a Sunday afternoon Sunday school at the near-by colored settlement of Eatonville.

Some ten or fifteen of us organized a Young Woman's Christian Temperance Union, meeting once a month in the parlor in Cloverleaf. There was then living near Orlando an English couple by the name of Lord and Lady Drury-Lowe. He was cousin of Lord Curzon, and she was a prominent worker in the W.C.T.U., a close associate of the head of the British branch. She came to Rollins and talked to us and in May of 1899 invited us to her house for afternoon tea. Some eight or ten of us hired a big wagon to take us. Lady Drury-Lowe showed us two or three rooms that were a veritable museum of things from all over the world where they had traveled. Then Lord Drury-Lowe guided us on a tour of the maze of trails cut through the virgin hammonck. All I remember of lunch was fennel sandwiches, something I had never heard of before, but she said, commonly used in England. We sang as we rode back to Rollins in the moonlight through the untouched forest.

We had debating societies and glee clubs, and all the other usual activities for youngsters our age, but no sororities or fraternities. On Friday nights Miss Pelton gave an entertainment using student talent, for which she charged an admission fee of five cents. I remember that one time they put on a little play in which Edith Foulkes was the leading lady and a minuet was danced.

The music department at that time was said to be the best Conservatory of Music south of Baltimore. Its graduating pupils gave individual concerts each year. The whole department gave three each year. The Dinky Line, whose tracks crossed the campus along the lake shore, ran a special train to bring folks from Orlando.

I belonged to the Chorus Club. We sang a variety of music, both religious and secular, but all good. The hours spent in practice were heaven to me. At that time piano and violin were the only instruments taught. The last year guitar and mandolin had been added. In addition to numerous upright practice pianos scattered in Knowles Hall, dining-room, Lyman Gymnasium and Cloverleaf, on the platform in the gym, which was the biggest auditorium on the campus, were a Steinway grand and a Chickering grand.

The two years Miss Anita Bibbins was head of the Department, for fifteen minutes at the close of chapel three mornings each week she taught us sight reading and musical interpretation. I think we learned every tune in the hymnbook.

CHAPTER X

FACULTY AND STUDENTS

Our first Cuban students came in the fall of 1897. Their immense wealth had all been confiscated by the Spaniards, except one diamond ring. Senora Gonzalez and the four children, Eulogio, about seventeen, Trina, about fifteen, Jacinto, thirteen, and Trina, eleven, stayed there at least two winters. Senora Gonzalez offered Dr. Ward the ring, but he refused to take it. He got friends of his in the North to provide for them, taking them North during the summer. Senor Gonzalez was imprisoned, and finally died of the hardships he endured. After the war the family were reunited in Havana. They were Cuban aristocrats, of pure Spanish blood.

Eulogio and Trina were old enough to have become very much the Cuban young gentleman and young lady, courtly manners and all. Jacinto and Fanny were soon indistinguishable from the Americans, language, slang, everything. Fanny was teaching Spanish at Rollins when I visited there in 1912.

At the same time there was another Cuban lady, equally cultured and charming, and her two little boys, aged about ten and twelve. Her wealth, too, had been confiscated. She still had a little Paris perfume, and showed me a Worth red silk evening dress and a gray flannel suit made by an equally famous London tailor. When I graduated from the Academy, she gave me a white feather fan, that I cherished until the moths ate it.

After the war so many Cubans came that the Americans were learning Spanish instead of the Cubans learning English. After that the number was limited to twenty at any one time. We had two boys from Ybor City. Most of the rest were from Havana and its environs. Dean Hills wrote the parents every week an account of their progess and welfare. I learned to take and transcribe his Spanish dictations as easily and accurately as English.

Of the faculty I remember only those I took classes under. Funny things were always happening. In our Latin class, not one of the six or seven boys and girls had properly prepared the lesson. One after another stumbled and sat down. Grace Jones started hesitantly, "Caesar saw . . ." By that time Prof. Austin's patience was worn out, and he snapped, "Well, **what** did he saw?" The time was up, so I didn't have to make a display of my ignorance.

Dr. Baker invited all of us in the dininghall at dinner to come to his classroom to view the circulation of blood through the tail of a batrachian. Someone asked, "What's that?" Sara Moses volunteered confidently, "Oh, that's the botanical name for a tadpole."

One time Dr. Ward dictated something about the ladies' diaphanous dresses. I got it "Daphneous." In his amusement, and to my chagrin, he wouldn't let me correct it, but sent it on to New England. But I learned a new word the hard way, as folks say nowadays.

Warm memories cluster about all of them. But I am grateful to Miss Alice Rich, a piano teacher, for her unfailing courtesy in answering my questions as fully as if I had been a paying pupil. And to Miss Susan Longwell, who held the chair of English and History. And to Miss Nathalie Lord, the secretary of the college. We used the typewriter which stood in her room. She had me read to her every paper I had to prepare for my various classes. I did not know it at the time, but found out after her death, that she was the teacher who taught Booker T. Washington to read and write and gave him the elocution lessons that helped make him one of the foremost orators of America. She was also my Sunday school teacher. I corresponded with her as long as she lived.

All those I came in contact with were friendly and interested, and gave me invaluable lessons outside the classroom. I think about the happiest Christmas Day I ever spent was with Dr. Baker in his makeshift laboratory, a little one-room board-and-batten building connected to Pinehurst by a covered board walk. He was experimenting with a new method of distilling camphor. Camphor trees had just been introduced into Florida. He used a little kerosene stove for heat. The process worked. At least the camphor distilled. The drawback was that the crystals collected on the sides of the square pipe he had made from ½″ x 2″ board nailed together, instead of going on to the receptacle prepared for them, so it had to be torn apart to get them.

He was a most versatile man. He was head of the Natural Sciences department, teaching natural philosophy and using a textbook he had written himself, chemistry, zoology, botany and astronomy. He taught German at least once when Prof. Hills was sick. He taught math when that teacher was absent. His delight was to take a flock of young folks on exploration trips. He took the botany class I was in around the west end of Lake Virginia. He led a group of boys who tried to measure the depth of the water in a sink hole about five miles from the college. The bottom was never discovered.

Miss Alice Merrill, the Rollins housekeeper, was very up to date in home economics. She gave me a copy of GOOD HOUSEKEEPING MAGAZINE. It was about 5½ x 8 inches, and had about forty pages. She followed its recommendations for balanced meals, as well as its ads. Several of our everyday foods were newcomers on the market. She served us Jello that the boys called, "nervous pudding."

I never thought about the ages of the faculty. But in talking with Dr. Ray Beyer one day when we were both in our fifties, he exclaimed, "How **young** they all were!" President Ward was sixty-six when he came there. Professor Hills was thirty-two. Professor Ford had grown daughters. Vice-president Morse proudly displayed the biceps he had developed rowing for Yale thirty years before. What was left of Dr. Baker's hair was snowy, but he had the carriage and vigor of a young man. Both Miss Nathalie Lord, the secretary of the College, and her sister, Frances Ellen Lord, the professor of Latin and Greek, had gray hair. Miss Nathalie's was abundant and snowy, inclined to wave. Both of them were young enough to have been charter members of the original Christian Endeavor Society that was organized February 1881. I don't suppose any of them were over fifty, even the oldest. But of them Dr. Ward said proudly, "My first faculty was unbeatable"; and Dr. Beyer said, speaking from the standpoint of a pupil, "Just to know them was a liberal education in itself."

When Knowles Hall burned all the original records were destroyed. I could give considerable help in reconstructing the list of students. I don't know how many of the earlier publications they were able to obtain. I personally know nothing of the founding of the college, except that it was by the Congregational organization in Florida. Many contributed to its endowment. A good bit of it was in orange groves, which at that time were considered about the equivalent of gold mines. The Big Freeze of '95 wiped all that out. When Dr. Ward took over in '96, the college was on financial rocks. Mr. Brewer came to the rescue by buying his estate for the $2,000 so desperately needed, far more than its value. Dr. Ward frequently walked into the office, slapping a sheaf of bills against his hand and saying, "Blessed be nothing, for then you can't lose it." By continued miracles of God's Providence, money to pay the bills came in.

I soon learned that although the love of money is a root of all kinds of evil, money itself is a commodity highly desirable to have in sufficient amount. I also learned that wealth does not protect from life's deepest sorrows. Of his five children, three were born dead, one lived about an hour, and one lived three days. That one was born in his father's home in Lowell, Massachusetts. When he walked into the office in Tampa where I was working, unable to speak, he silently held out the baby's picture. When Dr. Ward saw my first baby, he said, "Emma, you're rich."

Of the founders, I think the only one still in Winter Park was the Mr. Lyman for whom the gymnasium was named. He taught my Sunday school class the first year I was there.

An early catalog said only such rules would be imposed as a conscientious student would place on himself. Rules and regulations were few and reasonable, and infractions few. Two or three stand out in my mind, especially in view of the demonstrations and riots now rife in schools and colleges the world over.

One day a big portion of the students skipped classes and went on a picnic on the east side of the lake. Dean Hills went out, sauntered around among them, and got the names of every one. They were a completely subdued and thoroughly frightened bunch when they got back—in plenty of time for supper. For they knew they were not supposed to step off the campus during school hours, and visions of being sent home tramped through their heads. There was no repetition of the offense.

One morning a boy insulted one of the colored girls as she was coming to work at six o'clock. The girl told Miss Merrill. The boy was shipped home on the noon train. Announcement was made at chapel the next morning. There was no repetition of that offense, either.

The other one concerned a girl from Australia. After being refused permission, she went to the depot to see her foster parents as they passed through. At a faculty meeting it was decided she should be expelled. I knew some of the faculty thought she had shown waywardness on previous occasions. When Mr. Morse made the announcement at chapel, a few of the boys and a few of the girls hissed and booed. I reckon my face must have been like a thundercloud, for when I got to the office Mr. Morse asked why the students felt that way. I told him she was an orphan, that these people were the only ones she knew in this country and had befriended her, and in view of the fact that she would have been gone from the campus only fifteen or twenty minutes and missed no classes, and would not have entered the train but stood beside it, we felt the rules should have been waived. He listened thoughtfully, without comment. The next morning he stood quietly until the commotion subsided. Then he said he would have felt the same way if it had been one of his own children, that disobedience was a serious thing. His moral courage made a deep impression on all of us.

During my years at Rollins I do not recall any students whose parents could be called wealthy, though many if not most were comfortably well off. Dean Hills wrote someone that the ones who were working their way were among the best students. I thought to myself, "Naturally, for they are here because they want an education, and are willing to work hard to get it." We had a few, a very few, who were wild or lazy, but it could truly be said that most of them were earnest, conscientious, and diligent. As Mary Burrell said, in a toast at a banquet honoring President Hamilton Holt, "Rolilns was a place where it was easy to do and be your best."

Many went on to distinction in medicine, education, law, the ministry. Ray Beyer told me about a heart operation he had performed five days before, saying with deep satisfaction, "They can no longer say it is one hundred percent fatal, for if the boy dies now it will be from something besides the operation." That operation put him in the forefront of the world's surgeons. Orville MacDonald and

Beatrice Perkins were married by Dr. Ward in his parlor, and went to Turkey under the American Board of Commissioners for Foreign Missions. Russell Barr became a Federal judge. Susie Gladwin and Louis Lyman were among the teachers sent to the Philippines by the United States after the Spanish-American War. Fred Ensminger, Harold Dale and Arthur Lincoln became Doctors of Divinity. All this and much more is in the archives of Rollins College, with no errors or omissions due to faulty memory.

The early catalog says of Rollins that its objective was to give an education that would enable the students to take a self-respecting place in the world. All fulfilled this ideal, for all took places of leadership in their own communities.

CHAPTER XI

WAR, TEACHING AND LIFE

I graduated from Rollins Academy in May, 1898. While Hon. Henry S. Chubb, the Republican leader in Florida, was giving the commencement address, Spanish-American War troop trains were whistling as they passed on their way to Tampa. As every year, it took me till Saturday to clear up the office work for the year. Moody and Sankey had held one of their revival meetings in Tampa during the winter. Mr. Sankey was returning to sing for the soldiers. He sat in the seat with me on the train. I have forgotten everything he said, but I remember what a big man he was, and how pleasant he was. That night he sang in a big open tabernacle on Florida Avenue two or three blocks north of Columbus Drive. The building was crowded. He had his own folding organ, and among other songs he sang THERE WERE NINETY AND NINE ,telling us how he had sung it the first time, in England. On the train to Scotland Mr. Moody had asked him if he could sing something new that night. He had in his pocket a newspaper clipping with the words that he sang that night, composing the music as he went along, the tune that became known around the world. It was a thrilling experience to me.

When I walked into church Sunday morning, Mr. Smith handed me his business card, with an office address where I was to call. Monday morning I went to work in the office of the Commissary Department of the United States Army, Major Abiel Leonard Smith in charge. He was without exception the most efficient boss I ever worked for. When he took over, essential food and supplies were in freight cars scattered from Lakeland to Port Tampa. In three weeks he had them straightened out and supplies flowing in promptly. He was equally efficient in the office. He said "Good morning" when he came in, the only irrelevant word all day. He got things done. He was a West Pointer, and gave me a profound respect for that institution.

Every day he dictated a letter often humorous to his two young sons. To his wife he wrote in his own handwriting. Most of the office detail was left to the chief clerk. He worked so hard and such terrific hours that once in a while he would put his head down on his desk and sleep ten or fifteen minutes, then go at it again. I learned a little of the work involved in running a war. Major Smith was promoted to Lieutenant Colonel and was sent to Puerto Rico, in charge of the expedition's Commissary Department. The last I heard of Colonel Smith he was a Brigadier general, retired.

While I was with the Commissary Department, another girl from our church was working on the floor below (each department occupied most of a whole floor of the First National Bank Building) for the Quartermaster's Department. She was Presco Cummings, a widow only five or six years older than I. I think she and I were the forerunners of all the WACs and WAVES, the first women to work in the United States armed forces while they were in the field in time of war.

Although I was working in the office of the Commissary Department, I saw virtually none of the military activity going on all around town. I had to be in the office before it started in the morning, remaining in the building all day, and going home before the nighttime social activity started. The townspeople opened their homes to the soldiers. Girls, enthusiastically utilized the opportunity.

I did not even see Teddy Roosevelt or Clara Barton. One day a very handsome tall soldierly man came into the office. After he had gone, one of the seventeen men in the office told me it was General Leonard Wood. Once I caught a glimpse of General Shafter as the horses struggled to pull his carriage up through the sand on Cline's Hill. I filed one letter signed with the utterly illegible squiggle of Arthur MacArthur.

Moody and Sankey in their evangelistic campaign that spring brought their own songbook, in which were copyrighted many of our best loved gospel hymns. Among the new ones was GOD BE WITH YOU TILL WE MEET AGAIN. It was sung on every possible occasion, especially those where soldiers were present. It expressed the desire of our hearts for those young men.

The end of the war closed the office in time for me to return to Rollins at the beginning of the term. I did not realize until long afterwards how Dr. Ward accommodated his office hours to enable me to take the classes I needed. He said jokingly that I had ruled his life, and I realized with a shock that that was pretty much the case. My courses were all mixed up in order to get classes at times that would suit us both. So when circumstances beyond my control compelled me to drop out in what should have been the junior year, I had taken some senior courses and omitted some freshman. But I want to take this opportunity to pay tribute to those at Rollins who so powerfully influenced my life for good.

Of those who influenced me most, the ones with whom I came most in contact were Dr. Ward himself, Prof. E. C. Hills, Dr. Thomas R. Baker, Prof. Susan Longwell, Miss Nathalie Lord, the college secretary, and Miss Alice Merrill, the housekeeper. They taught me how to study, how to redeem the time as well as its value, and by precept and example instilled in me the highest Christian principles. I can truly say I thank God for them.

I notice that in some places I have spoken of President George Morgan Ward as Mister and sometimes as Doctor. In the spring of

1897 he was given the degree of Doctor of Divinity by Dartmouth College, his alma mater. That fall the first morning I greeted him as Mister, and he said, "Doctor from now on," then went on to say his father had been a dentist and that he himself had been "Doc" all his life.

I also want to pay tribute to those men and women who out of self-sacrificial Christian generosity gave to the impersonal cause of education, that the boys and girls of Florida might get the educational opportunities they otherwise would not have had. I never knew even the names of many of them, and I am sure they did not know mine; but the last week I was at Rollins I copied the names and addresses of five hundred whom Vice President Oliver Cromwell Morse expected to interview that summer in behalf of Rollins.

One of the memorable events of my years at Rollins was the State Christian Endeavor convention in March, 1898. What proved to be a pivotal religious movement with worldwide impact began February 2, 1881, when a young Canadian minister, pastor of the Williston Congregational church of Portland, Maine, originated and organized the first Young People's Society of Christian Endeavor. Francis Edward Clark became known affectionately to millions as Father Endeavor Clark. The idea was flexible and adaptable, and spread through all denominations in all countries. At one time the northernmost society was at Point Barrow, Alaska, with one of two thousand members "right where the Congo crosses the equator." It was designed as a training school for young converts. The core of the pledge was never changed: "Trusting in the Lord Jesus Christ for strength, I promise Him I will strive to do whatever He would have me do," and "to take some part aside from singing in every prayermeeting." Many future civic leaders learned to "think on their feet" and to speak in public. Herbert Hoover was a president of his home society in Oregon.

My sister Minnie and her future husband, John Clifford Sayre, were charter members of the first Society in this area, in the First Congregational church of Tampa. Almost simultaneously one was organized in the First Presbyterian church of Tampa and in the Congregational in St. Petersburg. The state convention in Winter Park in 1898 brought delegates from all parts of the state. Those from Key West came by steamer to Tampa. Those from Pensacola went to Jacksonville by the Louisville & Nashville Railroad, from there to Winter Park by the Plant System. How those from Coconut Grove got there I don't know, but there was at least one present.

Meetings were held in a big tent seating four or five hundred. The music was under the direction of the Rollins music department. The ladies quartette sang every day, introducing, among others, such favorites as "Come On The Wings Of The Morning" and "Under His Wings."

The principal speaker was Dr. Clark, who had just returned from a trip around the world. There were several other distinguished speakers, among them Dr. Ira Landrith of Nashville. Dr. Clark and Dr. Landrith were put up at the Seminole Hotel. Other delegates were accommodated elsewhere, many of them in Rollins dormitories. All were fed at Rollins, in relays. The dininghall seated one hundred and twenty. One night Dr. Clark was there as the guest of the Misses Frances and Nathalie Lord, who had been charter members of the original society. I was one of several students Miss Merrill had helping wait on table.

The winter of 1901-02 stands out in my memory for several reasons. It was the first term of school I taught. My nerves had given way under the strain of working my way and keeping up with my college studies, and if I worker in the afternoon I ran a typewriter all night in my sleep. So I went to Prof. Graham, then the county superintendent of schools, and asked if I would be allowed to teach without having had normal training. He replied briefly, "If you can pass the examination." I bought some textbooks on the way home, only to find when I got there that Ma was sick, so that for three days and nights I did not undress. That left me three days in which to prepare for examination on subjects I had not thought about for five years. I managed to get a passing grade, though Prof. Graham said, of my arithmetic, "I'm ashamed of you, Emma." There were only three schools left in the county to which teachers had not been assigned. I chose the one I thought would give me the quietest time. The Lord was guiding me, for I went to board with the W. B. Moodys, and under their loving care I soon recovered my health completely. The children were small, none over the fifth grade, well behaved and good students. It was a pleasant winter for me.

Elsie Dickenson, another Tampa girl, taught the nearest school, three miles from mine. For Christmas we thought we would hold a combined celebration of the two schools. She brought her little flock to my school and I took mine to hers for rehearsals. On Saturday before Christmas we met at the Simmons home where she was boarding. The girls sewed the net socks and the boys filled them with the nuts and candy they had bought in Tampa. Christmas Day, Wednesday, some of her boys went out with a yoke of oxen and brought in the most symmetrical short-leaved pine I have ever seen used for a Christmas tree. It was also the largest. We held the celebration in an isolated log building I was told was a Primitive Baptist church. The tree was more than half as wide as the room, and reached to the peak of the roof. Her young folks decorated it lavishly with tinsel and ornaments and candles. It was breath-takingly beautiful.

Although it had frozen Saturday morning so that for the only time in my life I saw little ice "fingers" in the mud (the weather bureau says it was the record cold for that date), by Wednesday the weather was so warm Elsie said, "Let's wear our summer dresses," which in those days meant white ones. Mine was dimity. All I remember about them is that I wore pink ribbon at throat and waist. We hung quilts on the north and west walls to shut the wind off from blowing out the lamps and candles.

We had a carefully planned program. I read Luke 2:8-20. We sang "Joy To The World," Fred Bravo accompanying us on his mouth organ. Then followed a half hour of songs and recitations by pupils of both schools. All I remember is the last line of one by one of my little girls, telling of the tribulations of learning to sew, and concluding with the paintive query, "And does it (the thread) get all brownish, too?" Santa Claus had a Spanish moss beard, and distributed the gifts in great style.

A few days earlier one of my boys had come to me shyly and said, "My Maw says to tell you she is forty-three years old and ain't never seed a Christmas tree, and to ask you if it would be all right for her to come?" I assured him we would be very glad to have her come, and that everyone was invited. When I stepped into the building that night, I was astonished. It had a few backless hewn log benches that would seat somewhere around fifty or sixty. Not only was every bench crowded, there was scarcely standing room left. I estimated the crowd at between one hundred twenty-five and one hundred fifty, with some standing outside. (The cracks between the logs permitted very good views of the inside). I was told there were people there who had come from ten miles away in ox wagons. What a dazzling vision they carried home with them, that warmed their hearts as long as they lived. I know it has mine.

The best of it all was that it showed them a better way to celebrate Christmas than the customary one of discharging fireworks and firearms and drinking until they were rowdy and quarrelsome.

Another memory of that winter that stands out was that in September the boys came back from noon recess with the news of President McKinley's assassination and death, which had been told them by the rural mail carrier as he passed on his way to Bradenton.

At that time teachers were required to take examinations every year, a custom which Prof. Bucholz complained bitterly "made his teachers eat stale bread." So when my school was out the last of February, I went back to Rollins to take the refresher course they were giving that year. It had been in progress several weeks. I started my algebra review with quadratic equations of two or more unknown quantities. The examination held here in Tampa was in June. The very first question was factoring at sight. I could have worked it out, but the instructions were strictly **at sight,** my mind went blank, and I left the answer blank.

When we had finished we were permitted to go out in the hall and talk to others all we wanted to. The last question was one of the X/y problems that look so deceptively simple. Someone asked May Smith how she had worked it. She replied airily, "Thus and so." My heart went to my heels. I knew May was brilliant and ranked high as a teacher. If she was right, then I was wrong, and could not possibly get a higher grade than eighty. With Prof. Graham's sorrowful "I'm ashamed of you" still fresh in my mind, worse than low grades was the thought of hurting my beloved teacher by having one of his star algebra pupils fail again. So when I got ninety, I knew May could not possibly get any more, which was a wee bit of salve to a bruised ego.

The examiners balanced the ninety-nine they gave me on physical geography with a lower mark than I expected on reading. For years I wondered idly what fault the lady found with it. It finally came to me that maybe she just possibly plain didn't like my Yankee accent. Intimate association with cultured New Englanders definitely affected my speech, which still betrayeth me.

A freeze was a pivotal event from which to date history. Most of the time the weather was so good people boasted, usually without contradiction, that it was the most wonderful climate in the world. We still have the same golden sunlight, the same gorgeous sunrises and sunsets, the same majestic thunderheads and crashing lightning and echoing thunder and refreshing rain, the same whole resplendent firmament on high declaring the glory of God, and reminding us we are still the recipients of His goodness and mercy.

Dear friends to whom my soul was knit, casual acquaintances whose lives barely touched mine in fleeting passing, all one by one have passed off the stage. Few are left who even faintly remember the conditions I have written about. The only thing I really miss is the profusion of wild flowers, the stately pines and shady roads, the giant oaks with their long swinging beards of gray moss, the bay-heads with their white flowering trees and tiny springs and crystal rills. I have tried to describe the things we used and did, to give a glimpse of the labors, the joys and the sorrows that filled our daily lives. I need only to mention all-electric kitchens, trans-world air-planes, television via Telstar, the satellite relay, and the space exploration achievements, to point up the difference between now and then. The man in the moon has been visible for eons, but a man on the moon is something altogether new and different.

I am thankful to have lived in just the period of the world's history I have. I am old enough to remember the good old days, and young enough to enjoy the far better new.